BASIC TEXTS IN COUNSELLING AND PSYCHOTHERAPY

Series editor: Stephen Frosh

This series introduces readers to the theory and practice of counselling and psycho-therapeutic skills and are particularly relevant to workers in health, education, social work and related settings. The books are unusual in being rooted in psychodynamic and systemic ideas, yet being written at an accessible, readable and introductory level. Each text offers theoretical background and guidance for practice, with creative use of clinical examples.

Published

Jenny Altschuler
WORKING WITH CHRONIC ILLNESS

Bill Barnes, Sheila Ernst and Keith Hyde
AN INTRODUCTION TO GROUPWORK

Stephen Briggs
WORKING WITH ADOLESCENTS AND YOUNG ADULTS 2nd Edition

Alex Coren
SHORT-TERM PSYCHOTHERAPY 2nd Edition

Jim Crawley and Jan Grant
COUPLE THERAPY

Emilia Dowling and Gill Gorell Barnes
WORKING WITH CHILDREN AND PARENTS THROUGH SEPARATION AND DIVORCE

Loretta Franklin
AN INTRODUCTION TO WORKPLACE COUNSELLING

Gill Gorell Barnes
FAMILY THERAPY IN CHANGING TIMES 2nd Edition

Fran Hedges
AN INTRODUCTION TO SYSTEMATIC THERAPY WITH INDIVIDUALS

Fran Hedges
REFLEXIVITY IN THERAPEUTIC PRACTICE

Sally Hodges
COUNSELLING ADULTS WITH LEARNING DISABILITIES

Linda Hopper
COUNSELLING AND PSYCHOTHERAPY WITH CHILDREN AND ADOLESCENTS

Sue Kegerreis
PSYCHODYNAMIC COUNSELLING WITH CHILDREN AND YOUNG PEOPLE

Ravi Rana
COUNSELLING STUDENTS

Tricia Scott
INTEGRATIVE PSYCHOTHERAPY IN HEALTHCARE

Geraldine Shipton
WORKING WITH EATING DISORDERS

Laurence Spurling
AN INTRODUCTION TO PSYCHODYNAMIC COUNSELLING 2nd Edition

Paul Terry
COUNSELLING AND PSYCHOTHERAPY WITH OLDER PEOPLE 2nd Edition

Jan Wiener and Mannie Sher
COUNSELLING AND PSYCHOTHERAPY IN PRIMARY HEALTH CARE

Shula Wilson
DISABILITY, COUNSELLING AND PSYCHOTHERAPY

Steven Walker
CULTURALLY COMPETENT THERAPY

Jessica Yakeley
WORKING WITH VIOLENCE

Invitation to authors

The Series Editor welcomes proposals for new books within the Basic Texts in Counselling and Psychotherapy series. These should be sent to Stephen Frosh at the School of Psychology, Birkbeck College, Malet Street, London, WC1E 7HX (e-mail s.frosh@bbk.ac.uk)

Basic Texts in Counselling and Psychotherapy
Series Standing Order ISBN 0–333–69330–2
(*outside North America only*)

You can receive future titles in this series as they are published by placing a standing order. Please contact your bookseller or, in the case of difficulty, write to us at the address below with your name and address, the title of the series and the ISBN quoted above.

Customer Services Department, Macmillan Distribution Ltd, Houndmills, Basingstoke, Hampshire RG21 6XS, England

WORKING WITH FATHERS

From Knowledge to Therapeutic Practice

JENNIFER WALTERS

Consultant Clinical Psychologist,
East London NHS Foundation Trust, London UK

palgrave
macmillan

First published 2011 by
PALGRAVE MACMILLAN

Palgrave Macmillan in the UK is an imprint of Macmillan Publishers Limited,
registered in England, company number 785998, of Houndmills, Basingstoke,
Hampshire RG21 6XS.

Palgrave Macmillan in the US is a division of St Martin's Press LLC,
175 Fifth Avenue, New York, NY 10010.

Palgrave Macmillan is the global academic imprint of the above companies
and has companies and representatives throughout the world.

Palgrave® and Macmillan® are registered trademarks in the United States,
the United Kingdom, Europe and other countries.

ISBN 978–0–230–21974–8

This book is printed on paper suitable for recycling and made from fully
managed and sustained forest sources. Logging, pulping and manufacturing
processes are expected to conform to the environmental regulations of the
country of origin.

A catalogue record for this book is available from the British Library.

A catalog record for this book is available from the Library of Congress.

10 9 8 7 6 5 4 3 2 1
20 19 18 17 16 15 14 13 12 11

Printed in China

For my father and mother, and Enid Marshall who was both mother and father to me.

CONTENTS

CONTENTS

Acknowledgements

I would like to acknowledge first all the fathers and their narratives without which I could not have written this book. I am indebted to them for their openness in telling their many stories.

I would also like to acknowledge and thank my many colleagues, friends and family members who have supported and encouraged me in this endeavour. As a busy practitioner it has been hard to find sufficient time to do justice to this work and the many shortcomings reflect this. I could not of course have completed the book without the constant and careful support and guidance from Stephen Frosh (series editor) and Catherine Gray (publisher) to both of whom I am extremely grateful.

ACKNOWLEDGMENTS

INTRODUCTION

My interest in fathers ostensibly began when I was working as a clinical psychologist in a small children's hospital in London's East End. I had begun to think particularly about men and loss following sessions with two fathers who had wept during the interviews, one about his stillborn child, born several years previously, and another about the death of his mother, also some years before. My impression is that we saw fewer fathers in clinic sessions then than now and although we were very familiar with depression in mothers, the presentation in fathers was much more unusual. Indeed, in the case of these fathers, they had never really talked about their painful losses to anyone.

These cases set me thinking firstly about men and loss but then about fathers' depression and the effects it might have on the family. Both the fathers mentioned above had boys who were soiling and they were also spending long hours away from the family and drinking, a common way for men to deal with depression. Interestingly it was notable how the symptoms in their sons began to improve following the fathers being able (or allowed) to talk about their great sadness. I began to think much more about the possibility of engaging fathers in clinical work with their families and how to go about this. So often we think about the mothers and their stories and indeed they are the parents who most commonly come to our clinics and hold the family history. But I was aware that fathers may be more willing than we expect to participate and that it is just as a result of habit that we pay more attention to mothers. These ideas began an interest in the engagement of fathers which led to several years of research and continues now in my clinical practice.

Margaret O'Brien was also a big influence on me and gave me vital encouragement in my work. She had written papers in 1988 and 1994 on men in therapy and 'the complex gendered patterning in the way humans recognise and communicate personal and family malaise' (1994, p. 19). Many women are able to seek help quite early on when experiencing depression but men tend to wait until individual or family stress has escalated to higher levels before taking action. Other authors (Jourard, 1971; Briscoe, 1982) echo this.

Sebastian Kraemer was also writing about the 'fragile male' (2000) and gave me crucial encouragement to carry out my research and the courage to write a paper (Walters, 1997). Kraemer argues that males are genetically more vulnerable from the beginning of life.

Other authors have influenced and inspired me. Charlie Lewis and I both studied with John and Elizabeth Newson, and Charlie encouraged me to link up with Margaret O'Brien. Vicky Phares, Arlene Vetere, Lawrie Moloney, Brid Featherstone, and Eirini Flouri have all written key texts on fatherhood. More recently Ramachandani has provided us with an excellent summary overview on fathers. Michael Lamb has of course written about and edited the seminal text on fatherhood.

The Fatherhood Institute in the UK has a remarkable website with information on every conceivable aspect of fathering. The research database meticulously constructed and maintained by Adrienne Burgess is an invaluable resource for any researcher in this area.

It was only as I was doing my research and interviewing 90 fathers about their children and their own parenting from their fathers that I began to realise more forcefully the relevance of my own history with my father. In some ways it was a painful realisation that made me reflect about intergenerational sorrow and how even when it is not expressed it percolates down in unconscious ways. I was the first of four children born to an older father who was 48 when I was born. He was something of a remote figure and worked long hours but I was nevertheless very close to him and remember many good times together when I was younger. Sadly he died when I was 16. I knew little of his history, just that his own father had died before I was born. Perhaps my memory is sketchy but I remember him telling me nothing of the truth about his father, who had left my father and his sister when my father was six. My father was born in 1900 and for a family to be left without a father at this time was particularly shameful. My grandmother refused to divorce him, so the story goes. It was a great surprise, therefore, when my father died that his half-brother, who had seen the notice in the paper, emerged. I had never known of this family, my grandfather's second family. It was remarkable to find cousins I had never known existed. I have even been in contact with more of them very recently as their mother, now dead, would not allow them to know of our existence because she was born illegitimate as a result of the fact that my grandfather was unable to remarry. In 2009, for the first time, I saw a photograph of my paternal grandfather.

As far as I know, my father never saw his father again after the age of six. My mother, some years later, told me of the existence of a letter kept by my father from his father in the 1930s asking him to meet with him. I now have this letter. It is accompanied by a note from my grandmother urging my father not to meet him. My father had grown up very close to his mother and must have felt that to meet his father would be a deep betrayal. I remember my mother (now also dead so I am unable to ask more) telling me that he always regretted not meeting his father at this time.

I suppose I reflect how, even though I have only learned much of the story in later life, something about the importance of fathers was around for me throughout. The story has filtered through to emerge in a strong research and clinical interest in the field and I would like to think that my father's sadness and loss and that of many like him has emerged to effect some changes in how we work with fathers present or absent and to promote their influence and importance.

This book has a wide remit and cannot cover everything in the detail it might deserve. However, it attempts to look at the salient issues for practitioners who are working with families in many settings but particularly the social and clinical fields. It is hoped that it will be relevant to those working in child and family settings, whether it be nurseries, schools or clinics of various kinds, and also social service settings.

A major difficulty is trying to find a unifying theme for a book of this kind. Fathers differ as much as anyone else and there are myriad fathering roles which vary according to culture, social class and work status, and whether the fathers live with or without their children. I have attempted to cover these topics and those of other roles such as stepfathers, gay fathers, fathers in prison, and so on. Fathers may have disabilities or mental health problems and these are also referred to. Fathering roles also vary according to age and so young fathers are another group to be discussed. The changes in the concepts of fathering over time are also an important topic.

In this book I have tried to think of the engagement of fathers as a predominant theme but within this simply to raise awareness of the importance of fathers in our work. Even when absent they should still be there in our minds as they are in the minds of the families we work with.

Fathers are also neglected in research, as will be shown later. In 2010 I attended a lecture on anxiety in children and the role of mothers. The lack of research into the influence of fathers at this time seems an extraordinary omission. There was a tide of research regarding fathers in the 1970s and 1980s and much of this work was very important in heralding the social changes in families. You will see that I lean quite heavily on some of the research from this time and also from the 1990s. Although research has continued there are still considerable gaps and it is sad to hear of projects in the twenty-first century which refer to mothers or parents but not specifically to fathers.

'In his own mind no child is "without a father". In the absence of a given story he will make up his own' (Kraemer, 2005). Kraemer goes on to make the point that if a father is entirely absent the child may never hear positive stories about him. He underlines the need to keep some positive stories alive, however small, so that the picture of a 'bad man' is not fully incorporated into the child's image of himself. The therapeutic task, says Kraemer, is to understand the missing father, to make sense of the story.

From a clinical perspective I enjoy working from an attachment and narrative theoretical base (Dallos, 2006) when thinking about fathers in families. Almost every day of my working life I see children and their families where there are issues, spoken or unspoken, about fathers. Some fathers attend appointments with their children, especially when a specific invitation has been made. Other fathers may be absent owing to work commitments. Some fathers are out of the picture entirely and not in touch with the family. Some fathers are in prison; some are living elsewhere but seeing their children. Some have injunctions against them. Whatever the situation, the importance of the father in the children's lives cannot be ignored. It is nonetheless remarkable how clinicians may still, even when the father is in the room, defer to the mother for information about the child. Where he is absent from a clinical session, asking about him can be forgotten completely. Sometimes this is because clinicians feel that it might be a difficult topic for the mother or children to talk about. Will questions create an upset, revive unpleasant memories or cause anger or sadness?

I was very struck by a conversation I had with a head teacher who decided to try to encourage the fathers of the children in her school, predominantly African Caribbean, to become more involved in their children's lives and education. She invited them in and to those who came she gave a quiz which included questions about the size of their children's shoes, the name of their teacher, and so on. The fathers went away and the need to find out this information of necessity led to them engaging more with their children. The children, she reported, were very excited by this involvement and it was the start of a successful project. It is by showing an interest in fathers that we can encourage their interest in their children. For many it is of course there without question but sadly for some the importance needs highlighting. That is not to say, however, that all fathers must engage with their children in any prescriptive way. Fathering can take many forms and it is the narrative or stories of positive involvement that children make of their fathers that are important. My own father, for example, for many reasons spent little time with me but I hold fond memories of the times we had and always felt he had me in mind. However, because I lost him when relatively young he was an idealised image for many years and it is only in later life that I have been able to see him in a more balanced light as a person who, like anyone else, had strengths and limitations.

This book, therefore, does not set out to extol the virtues of fathers as essential to children's upbringing. There is of course much research to support the importance of fathers in children's development (Lamb, 2004). But the situation is more complex and especially in our rapidly changing postmodern world. There is a myriad of different family structures and the two-parent heterosexual couple is less likely to be the norm in the West. Several writers (Perlesz, 2005; Silverstein and Auerbach, 1999) are questioning the need for fathers in families, citing evidence that children can grow up successfully in a variety of family structures. These authors state that 'children need at least one responsible, caretaking adult who has a positive emotional connection with them, and with whom they have a consistent relationship' (Silverstein and Auerbach, 1999. p. 3). Tasker and Golombok's work on lesbian parenting echoes these views.

I am therefore setting out to explore the meaning of fathers to their children in whatever culture or family constellation they may reside. Many men in my generation grew up with fathers who had either fought in the war or had done national service. For these men emotional commitment was probably hard, given that one might have to become separated from loved ones in situations that were life-threatening. Moloney (2002) touches on these issues and also poignantly describes the story of his grandfather and his role as a father over the years, the stories he never told of loss and the need to relocate for work, and his death 'too young', leaving Maloney wondering whether he 'simply felt there was nothing left for him to do' (2002, p. 72). Most men who have children do not now have to think of going off to fight. Ironically, however, much looser family structures have now replaced the former situation where family solidity was the rockbed of stability.

There is no doubt that fathers are much higher on the political agenda now than they used to be. In recent years I have attended meetings on fathers' rights, Muslim fathers, fathers in education, and fathers and parenting. Several factors have influenced this change and the emergence of women in the workforce is one of the most significant. There are many more single-parent families, mostly headed by mothers, but other families have experienced increases in father participation. Increasing cultural diversity has contributed to changing conceptualisations of the role of the father in the family (Cassano et al., 2006).

It is notable how theories of fathering, and mothering, are rooted in economic contexts. Bowlby's ideas on attachment, for example, were popular in the 1950s when mothers in this country were mostly at home with the children while the men were out at work. Unemployment for men was uncommon at this time. But we can easily forget how the surface bliss of family stability at that time was, for many women, masking serious problems of loneliness, mental underperformance and depression. Women had performed many roles during the war and day nurseries had been introduced for children as a result. However, after the war women were placed firmly back in the home, often perhaps to their detriment.

Theoretical models

I have worked for many years with children and their families and have encountered a number of theoretical models ranging from developmental, and behavioural through to cognitive behavioural, psychodynamic and systemic theories. After all this time I have developed my own style of working, and the models I find most comfortable and which carry the most meaning for me in my work tend to be around attachment and narrative. This is not to say that I do not work in other ways where I feel it necessary. Sometimes a cognitive behavioural approach is appropriate and at other times a neurodevelopmental approach is helpful. Where adult services tend to have specialists in different areas, working with children and families requires an open mind about how to work with families and for this reason workers need to have a variety of approaches up their sleeves. This is not, however, an excuse for superficiality. Workers need to be able to assess where their expertise begins and ends and where specialist therapies, treatments or consultations are required.

Men make up half of our population and they vary as much as anyone else, so there is no way in which a specific therapeutic approach can be prescribed for them. There are some guidelines regarding gender and therapy which I will mention in the chapters on engagement and mental health in men. Fathers are of course a subgroup of the male population and we will be working with them as part of a family, whether they are living with the family or not. However, fathers are also individuals with all their idiosyncrasies and so working with fathers on their own is sometimes appropriate, although much rarer in a child and family service. A combination of individual and family approaches therefore provides a very useful framework.

When working with fathers a systemic model is appropriate as we are thinking of them as part of a family, although in many disparate ways. But we are also thinking of fathers as individual adults with their own histories and patterns of attachments. They will in turn have their own narratives or stories to tell. They may also have problems such as anxiety, depression or substance use, or they may have learning difficulties or neurodevelopmental difficulties such as being on the autistic spectrum. As always in our work, all these aspects need to be kept in mind.

A particular model that I have found helpful in my clinical work is what could be called 'attachment narrative' therapy. This model is one espoused by Dallos (2006). Dallos helpfully describes the limitations of each theory, systemic, narrative and attachment, on their own and the advantages of a combined approach. He sees systemic theory and therapy as neglecting individual experience and lacking in a developmental perspective. He also suggests that systemic theory and therapy can neglect links between family patterns and problems. Attachment theory can be seen as overly biological and deterministic, focusing too much on dyads, particularly mother and child, and laying blame on mothers. He sees narrative theory as being shaped by emotional processes which may be distorted versions of events: 'An understanding of how they have learnt to place their experiences into narratives and the ways that they transform events, for example a pattern of excluding the contribution of feelings, attachments and relationships to their problems, may help our ability to talk and construct new narratives with families' (2006, pp. 8–9).

Systemic theory at its simplest works with families, looking at patterns of interaction in the group as a whole and how they affect each other. In particular, systemic therapists will tend to look at what is happening in the here and now and how it connects with belief systems in the family.

In his book Dallos describes the theoretical and research background of attachment theory and how attachment and narrative therapies can combine within a systems framework when working with families. This model is not of course specific to working with fathers. However, being cognisant of an attachment framework and stories around fathers and fathering is I find important for engagement and continuing work. In many instances, therefore, it is useful to think about a combination of family and individual or dyadic work.

Sarah and Len came with their son who was five to discuss his sleep problems. Jack was coming into their bed every night and often wetting the bed. If returned to his own bed he would scream for prolonged periods, which resulted in them always allowing him to sleep with them. Sarah and Len were exhausted and could not agree on a strategy to resolve the problems. Len worked long hours, the family had considerable debts, and the relationship was extremely poor. Len had already left the family on two occasions but financial problems had meant that he had had to return.

On several occasions Sarah came to see me either alone or with Jack. Len was working and often found it hard to get away. Sarah told of the difficulties in her relationship with Len and how they had met when relatively young and been together for several years before Jack was born. She came from a large family and had regular contact with her parents and siblings, who were all supportive. Jack had a lot of cousins.

Eventually Len asked to see me alone. The couple had been discussing separation and he was clearly finding it difficult. They had both decided that their relationship was not working but Len found it hard to move out. He broke down, describing how hard it was to leave their only child and saying that his own father had left when he was very young and how little contact he now had with him. We discussed the differences between his situation and his father's and how history did not have to repeat itself. In fact, there was every indication from him that he would not allow the same situation to arise and would be a far more committed father than his own. The very fact that he was seeking help in order to try to work out how he could make his separation from the family work well for his son showed how differently his father's departure from the family many years before had been handled.

For subsequent sessions the couple came together. Len had moved out, things were difficult financially and he seemed depressed. Sarah, however, looked much better and Jack's sleep had improved. He was spending one night a week at his father's and , although asking a lot of questions about his parents not being together, was showing signs of adapting to the situation in a way that he had not when Len had moved out before. Len and Sarah were enjoying the time they had together more than when they had lived together. However, it was clear that Len wanted some more individual work to help him. He had fewer family resources than Sarah and less of a sense of how to manage on his own in his role with Jack. It was suggested that Len might join a weekly therapy group for fathers and he took this up, although he was an irregular attender.

Work by John Byng-Hall (1995) on rewriting family scripts was an important development in using an attachment framework with families and creating in therapy a secure enough base from which family members can explore their own attachments. In many ways this work has been very important and a precursor to current theories on attachment narrative therapies.

Attachment theory and fathers

Much of the early work around attachment was focused on mothers. However, children have both a mother and a father and, although this is still not well researched, there is some work which teases out this more complex picture of attachments to both parents. The Adult Attachment Interview (AAI) is an interview used for research purposes which looks at narratives around early attachments to parents or parental figures. Work by Fonagy et al. (1994) shows how early events per se are not predictive of later behaviour but it is how they are perceived that is crucial. Fonagy et al. (1991) have carried out some important research looking at intergenerational risk using the AAI (George, Kaplan and Main, 1985). Their data suggest the existence of an intergenerational relationship between perceptions of one's own childhood experiences of being parented and the later parenting of one's own children. For both mothers and fathers, the association between a detached adult attachment pattern shown in the AAI and insecure child behaviour rated from the Strange Situation technique (Ainsworth, 1978), and free/autonomous adult attachment pattern and secure infant behaviour were the strongest. The pattern of concordance for fathers was weaker than that for mothers but still statistically significant. The authors do not comment on the relative importance of maternal and paternal attachment patterns, although it is noted by Holmes (1993) that maternal, rather than paternal, security is the more potent transmitter of secure attachment across the generations. This point is predicated upon maternal dominance of childcare and is questionable in the light of current findings on the importance of fathers and their possibly greater involvement in parenting. In a review of eleven studies using the Strange Situation classification paradigm, Fox et al. (1991) found consistent evidence for concordance between infant–mother and infant–father attachment styles. They suggest that parental dyads may show similar types of parenting behaviours which increase the likelihood of similar attachment to both parents. Fonagy et al. (1994) discusses the possible independent influence of the two parental working models and the security of the infant–parent relationship in the first 18 months of life: 'The strong association suggests that each parent "transmits" their internal working model independently of the actions of the other parent' (p. 240). It is not yet known at what stage the separate internal working models might become integrated to produce a general stance towards attachment relationships. It may be that some children can accommodate secure internal models beside a more insecure one from a stable and responsive figure and this may account for some children developing more resilient internal working models. The important point about Fonagy's work is that, despite the apparent determinist nature of the influence of early experience, there is potential for picking up those adults who are likely to transmit insecure models to their children and facilitate change through psychotherapeutic treatment focusing on reflection. Biringen (1994) points out the potential for assessment in therapy using measures of attachment before and after therapy which can be reliably and validly evaluated. In the setting of the family and child psychiatry clinic, mothers have often been the focus of work on attachment but far less so fathers. As fathers become more involved in nurturing roles with their children, it is important that this imbalance be redressed.

A therapeutic development deriving from the context of attachment relationships and theory of mind was developed by Allen and Fonagy (2006). This therapy, termed mentalisation-based therapy, originally applied to clients with personality disorders but is now being used more widely and basically helps clients to attend to or hold in mind states of mind in self and others. The practice of encouraging mentalisation in families is particularly poignant as 'these relationships characteristically provoke the most glaring impairments in mentalisation' (p. 261). Certainly these techniques can be used in both individual and systemic work although, as with all therapeutic models, they are not specific to men or fathers.

Dominant discourses and fathers

In every family there are stories and these are handed down through generations. Practitioners will often encounter narratives about men in the family, myths about how fathers behave, and so on: 'All the men in this family leave their wives eventually'; 'He never did anything to help with the children and neither did his own father'; 'There's no point in trying to change him, they're all the same', or, more positively, 'He's just like his dad, always wanting to play with the children and so good with them.' Where the stories are negative, and these are the situations we are most likely to meet, beliefs can and should be challenged. Why should the negativity continue through generations? Temperaments may be genetic and this can be hard to shift but behaviours are usually learned and respond to a context or an environment. No two situations are identical and choices can be made about how to behave and be in families. Of course we are all influenced by our parents but we can learn to take from our experiences what was good and adapt the rest. The task of therapy can be to elicit dominant stories and from there to gain different views and alternative stories, maybe extracting new information which may create exceptions to the dominant story. The therapist will then need to work hard to keep these alternative views alive and to embed them in the family beliefs.

Shabbir had always struggled with depression. His father and his brother also had a history of depression and a male cousin had committed suicide when he was in his early twenties. Shabbir was concerned that his son aged twelve, who was unhappy at secondary school, was going to be like the men in the family.

In fact, Shabbir's son had been very happy in primary school and it was only when he did not get a place in the secondary school of his choice that he became unhappy. All his friends had gone to another school and this school was not near home. He was on the waiting list for his first choice of school and indeed a place came up following a letter from the clinic. The boy settled well and was much happier being nearer to home and back with his old friends.

Shabbir was pleased with the result and we encouraged him to question the idea of his depression being heritable. In fact, his early life in another country and the struggles when his family were refugees were obvious factors in his mood. He began to understand and believe that his son had a different and more secure life with more stability and opportunities than Shabbir had had. He became less anxious about his son and even his own depression lifted somewhat when he was able to think that he might not have passed on the low moods to the next generation.

The book is divided into seven chapters which explore different aspects of fathers and fathering. It begins by examining demographic features of fathers, who they are, where they are, and how fathering as a concept has changed over the generations. Subsequent chapters look at men and parenting, men's mental health in relation to fathering, and the role of fathers. A chapter follows on the engagement of fathers in clinical work with families. Other topics include separated fathers, lone fathers, fathers in prison, domestic violence and fathers, working with fathers and men in groups, and cultural aspects of fathering.

The aim of this book is not so much a therapeutic guide but more a text to help practitioners keep fathers in mind in their work and to raise and demonstrate a strong awareness of fathers and their importance in children's lives, whether negative or positive. Too often fathers are ignored because they are absent or thought to be hard to engage. I would like to emphasise that workers do not necessarily need to be highly skilled in the various therapies to work with fathers. It is hoped, however, that the case vignettes contained within this text can provide some examples of thinking about fathers in relation to families and how to work with them in productive ways.

1

DEMOGRAPHY AND FATHERS

This chapter examines family structures and patterns of caretaking of children and how these have changed. When working with families we are often not meeting with the traditional nuclear family. The most common presentation will be a mother with her children but we are also working with fathers who are separated from their families, stepfathers, adoptive fathers, gay fathers, lesbian mothers and families from a variety of cultures. The need for flexibility and adaptability to these various constellations is paramount and within this the need to see the work with each family as unique. The second half of the chapter looks at some of the cultural aspects we need to be aware of when working with families.

One fifth of dependent children in Britain live with a single parent (Flouri, 2005). Of these, 2 per cent are lone-father families and 19 per cent lone-mother families. In the UK one in eight children before the age of 16 is likely to live in a family where the birth parent will have formed a new partnership. In the US one in three children will, before the age of 18, live with a step-parent who is usually a stepfather. These statistics underline the fact that fewer children are growing up in traditional households. Moreover, with more equality between men and women in the workforce, fewer households are likely to be supported by a single male earner. There has also been a big increase in the number of fathers who choose to stay at home while their partner goes out to work.

The proportion of households comprising a mother and a father with dependent children changed from 38 per cent in 1961 to 23 per cent in 2001. During this period lone-parent households increased. Nonetheless 80 per cent of dependent children live in two-parent families (compared to 92 per cent in 1972). 6 per cent of these have a step-parent.

A higher divorce rate and more cohabiting have influenced these demographic changes. It is the case that cohabiting relationships are more likely to break up than marriages. Unfortunately a high percentage (20–30 per cent) of non-resident fathers have not seen their children in the past year and another 20–40 per cent see their children less than once a week, but inevitably the amount of contact varies according to the age of the child, the length of the separation, and, in some studies, the gender of the child. Moreover, divorced fathers are at greater risk than married fathers of having problems with drink and drug use.

Abimbola separated from his partner when his children were 5 and 3. He made visits and took them out weekly but his ex-partner began to make this very difficult for him. She often said that the children were ill or tired and Abimbola found that he had to make great efforts to persist. Gradually weeks were missed and the children seemed more reluctant to see their father. He began to feel defeated and to give up. He also began to drink more and at one point rang his ex-partner when he was drunk. This gave her more reason to prevent the children from seeing him.

Abimbola still, however, sent them cards on their birthdays, although he did not know whether they received them. He also on occasions went to their school and, keeping out of their sight, watched them coming out so that he could see how they were growing and changing.

Statistics state that in the US 64.2 per cent of children are living with a biological mother and father, 22.7 per cent with a single biological mother, 2.5 per cent with a single biological father, 6.7 per cent with a biological parent and step-parent, and 3.9 per cent with no biological parent (Hofferth et al., 2002).

In terms of ethnicity, the percentages living with a single biological mother are 52.5 per cent for African-American children, 15.5 per cent for Caucasian children and 25.7 per cent for Hispanic/Latin/Latina children. Hofferth et al. (2002) states that 70–80 per cent of children who live with their single or divorced biological mother have some contact with their biological father.

In figures quoted from the Office for National Statistics survey from 2001, mothers account for more than three-quarters of the time spent on childcare activities during the week and two-thirds at weekends. On average fathers of under-fives spend 1 hr, 20 mins per day on childcare activities during the week and 2 hrs, 30 mins per day at weekends.

Hunt (2009) writing in a publication from the Family and Parenting Institute on Family Trends corroborates this and states that mothers still spend more time on childcare than fathers, although more fathers are involved in childcare than previously. In fact, working mothers spend more time with their children now than non-working mothers did in 1981. Labour-saving devices in the home have played a part in this. There is also a shift from parents seeing education as the school's responsibility to it becoming their responsibility.

Many parents seem to be reducing their personal and leisure time, including time spent on sleeping, and spending time with their children. Social class plays a large part in the division of labour in households. Where women are employed full time, for example, there is less of a traditional division of domestic labour. If women work full-time or earn more than their partners, then men do more of the routine work. Women with more education do less housework and men with more education do more. Attitudes towards housework are less traditional in professional and managerial households.

During the period 1974 to 2000 it was found that fathers were spending 200 per cent more time with their children (Hunt, 2009). This increase was particularly marked in fathers with very young children. Nonetheless the data is not unequivocal. Some researchers dispute the methodologies and say that there has not been such an increase in paternal involvement.

Paternal involvement is important. With regard to education it is likely to be higher with first-borns and where there are fewer siblings. Involvement is also greater where fathers are unemployed, retired or have a disability. Better relationships between partners are also a positive predictor. Interestingly, however, Washbrook (2007) found that where children in the early years spent 15 or more hours a week in their father's care the children had poorer scores on academic tests when they started school. It is possible, therefore, that in this particular group fathers may be monitoring their children but not necessarily engaging with them. How fathers spend time with their children is as important as how much time they spend with them. This does not, however, mean that 'quality' time is of the essence. Sometimes older children just need their parents to be there in the background rather than constantly engaging with them.

Renk et al. (2003) reviewed the literature on paternal/maternal roles. They looked at a university sample of parents. These families may have had less-traditional role theories as a result of being an academic population. The researchers found that neither the sex of the parent nor the gender role were predictive of the time parents spent in direct interaction with their children but that the sex of the parent qualified by earning status was predictive of levels of responsibility. This was perhaps a surprising finding given that most studies indicate that mothers spend more time with their children. However, when the results were analysed it was found that although mothers and fathers were spending approximately equal amounts of time with their offspring, mothers were taking more responsibility for child-related tasks such as homework, discipline, and caretaking and fun activities than were fathers. This meant that the primary responsibility was still with mothers. Parental satisfaction with child-related tasks was higher in fathers who reported higher levels of femininity on questionnaires.

Other studies have varying findings. Hofferth and Anderson (2003), for example, studied 2531 parents in US from a study in 1997. They looked at the engagement, availability, participation, and warmth of residential fathers in married biological parents, unmarried biological parents, married step-parents, and cohabiting father families. They found that biology explained less about father involvement than anticipated. Marriage differentiated paternal investment in that it was likely to be higher, and other variables differentiating investment were the age of the child and financial responsibility to non-residential children.

A US study by Yeung et al. (2001) looked at children's involvement with their fathers in intact families measured by time spent together. Fathers still do less of the parenting but fathers' involvement appears to be increasing. A 'new father' role for fathers at weekends is emerging with intact families. Different determinants of involvement were found. There is a negative relationship between father's work hours and wages and time spent with children in the week but this changes at weekends. A less-supportive work environment was found to be associated with lower levels of father parenting quality by Goodman et al. (2008). Their study was carried out on 446 low-income fathers in North Carolina and Pennsylvania. The study involved home visits and videotaped observations.

Several authors mention a lack of cultural studies of fathers. However, cultural studies find that black fathers are less involved and Latino fathers (Lamb, 2004) more involved with their children than are white fathers. This creates a more complex picture than a 'simple gender inequality theory' (see the section below on the cultural aspects of fathering).

Fathers in research

Phares (1996) notes that further research is needed on the determinants of fathers' participation in research studies as well as a detailed examination of the demographic representativeness of participating fathers in research. An early review from the 1970s by Rosenthal and Rosnow (1975) showed both male and female research participants to be more highly educated, of higher socio-economic status, more intelligent, more sociable and more in need of social approval than non-participants. These authors also found that adult women were more likely than adult men to participate in research (provided that it was not perceived as potentially stressful), supporting the supposition that in parenting research fathers were then more difficult to recruit than mothers. However, as Phares (1996) points out, it is difficult to say whether fathers are less willing to participate compared with mothers or whether in fact researchers' expectations of paternal participation is low and therefore fathers are less likely than mothers to be approached and recruited. A study by Hops and Seeley (1992) suggests that fathers who reported higher levels of depression were more likely to participate in research when their partners did not. Where only mothers and not fathers in two-parent families participated in research, Hops and Seeley found that the mothers reported lower levels of family cohesion and higher levels of marital dissatisfaction compared with other mothers.

A study by Phares (1995) comparing the fathers and mothers of college students examined the participation of both parents. Her study supported the conclusions reached by Woollett et al. (1982), who suggested that fathers were not harder to recruit than mothers. However, Phares's sample was well educated, and her research was perceived by parents to be helping their children indirectly. It has been noted (Graham, 1992) that much research is in this mode, and pays insufficient attention to ethnic diversity and lower socio-economic groups

Cassano et al. (2006) updated the area of inclusion of fathers in child psychopathology research. They looked at papers published from 1992 to 2005 which examined 'parental contributions to child psychological maladjustment'. Previous findings by Phares (1992) were replicated in that fathers continue to be neglected in child research, and the authors express their discouragement at this finding. However, there were indications that more father research was done as the age of the children increased. Paradoxically this meant that there were more fathers involved in research into adolescence where fathers are less likely to be living with their children. The authors suggest that research hypotheses such as those regarding substance use and paternal involvement may be one reason for this apparent anomaly. The authors also found that studies involving predominantly Caucasian samples showed separate analyses for mothers and fathers more often than those involving African-American samples. In this case the authors wondered whether the stereotype of African-American fathers being more likely to be absent might be relevant, despite research findings that African-American fathers may be as much involved as Caucasian fathers (Smith et al., 2005). Clinical journals were found by Cassano et al. (2006) to include more research involving fathers than developmental psychology journals.

Cassano et al. (2006) felt that researchers may still assume that fathers are difficult to recruit to research, despite these assumptions not being supported. Costigan and Cox (2001), however, suggest a self-selection bias in fathering research. Cassano et al. also suggest that research hypotheses may be based on outdated assumptions about who looks after the children and related tasks. They also state that it is relatively recently that policy makers have become interested in fathers and this is reflected in the levels of inclusion of fathers in research. Of those who participated in research from their study of 661 families, fathers who had less education, later-born children, more ambivalent marriages, more traditional child-rearing beliefs, less optimal parenting environments, unplanned children, children who were difficult temperamentally and children who were less healthy were underrepresented. Ethnic minorities and fathers of lower social class were also underrepresented.

Methodological issues arise with studies. Mikelson (2008) examines comparisons of maternal and paternal reports of father involvement which say that fathers report spending 17.6 per cent more time in activities with their children than mothers report. This is an interesting finding, showing that parents' perceptions differ, and it is essential for researchers to keep this in mind when comparing and reporting data.

I attended a conference where research in progress was presented on the relationship between mothers' anxiety and psychopathology in their children. The role of fathers was not included in this research and the presenter was clear that this was not the research interest. Phares et al. (2005, p. 736) has stated that 'there continues to be a dearth of research on fathers and developmental psychopathology. This pattern has not changed over the past 13 years ... Given that significant relationships are found between fathers and normative developmental issues (Lamb, 2004) and fathers and developmental psychopathology (Videon, 2005) there is a clear need to increase the inclusion of fathers in research related to child well-being.' This is an extraordinary and sad situation given our current world and the changes in the roles of fathers.

What do families look like now in the twenty-first century?

Flouri (2005) states that there has been a big increase in birth outside marriage in the UK and the European Union. However, there are wide variations, with the lowest percentage being in Cyprus (21 per cent) and the highest in Estonia (56 per cent). In the UK it is 40 per cent. Most births outside marriage are to cohabiting couples.

Statistics from the Office for National Statistics 2003 on social trends show that the divorce rate in the UK has risen from 2 per 1000 in 1960 to 13.6 per 1000 in 1995. There has therefore been a large increase in lone-parent families. Only 2 per cent of these are lone fathers and 19 per cent lone mothers. This has almost doubled since 1981. In the US a report by Ventura and Bachrach (2000) cites that in 1999 one third of births were to unmarried mothers compared with 4 per cent in the 1940s.

In the US it is predicted that half of all children will live with only one parent at some time during their childhood (up to the age of 16). In the UK, Dunn (2002) reports that this figure is one in eight for children who live in a family where there is one of their parents with a new partner. In the US one third of children before the age of 18 will be with a step-partner (usually biological mother and stepfather – Hofferth and Anderson 2003). Houses that are female-headed in the US have increased from 6 per cent in 1960 to 24 per cent in 1998. The highest rates of female-headed households are in some African countries and in Slovenia, Denmark, Finland. New Zealand and Sweden (Flouri, 2005). There has therefore been an increase in the numbers of children being raised in families not fitting the so-called conventional model of two biological parents.

In tandem with this there are more mothers in the workforce. In the UK in 1951, 26 per cent of married women were in paid labour. This contrasts with 71 per cent in 1991 (Walby, 1997), although this has since fallen slightly as a result of recession). It is unclear how many are in full-time or part-time work and this distinction is important when thinking about the effects on family life in terms of both the time involved and income. The directives on flexitime for workers are another important dimension in terms of the effects of working parents on family life. In 1991, households with a single male earner were 34 per cent of households with two adults. Cabrera (2000) reports that in the US the percentage of children living in two-parent families supported by a single male earner is approximately one quarter.

The rise of feminism is interlinked with economic change. Marsiglio et al. (2000) talk of 'fundamental shifts in family life, gender relations, men's declining wages, and increases in both women's participation in the paid labour force and men's involvement as primary nonmaternal care providers' (p. 1174). There is little doubt that the increasing number of women in the workforce has given women greater economic independence and thus the ability to maintain families without a male earner. However, the contribution of men to domestic labour has increased at a slower level than the increasing involvement of women in the workforce. Sandberg and Hofferth (2001) report that the average weekly time that children spent with their fathers increased very little between 1981 and 1997 but was more significant, unsurprisingly, in families where mothers were working outside the home. The Equal Opportunities Commission reports that fathers do a third of parental childcare, which is an eightfold increase in a generation for fathers of preschool children. The assertion that children spend less time with parents today as a result of mothers going out to work seems to be unfounded (Yeung et al., 2001). Unfortunately it is still the case that fathers' working hours in the UK are the longest in Europe. This is something that requires intervention at government level for significant change to occur. It will be interesting to see the possible effects of the financial crisis in 2008 in terms of the possible loss of jobs and changes in the hours of work for both men and women.

Anne who worked part time as a nurse was expecting her third child. Her partner was an architect whose job was threatened by the recession. She planned to return to work and to work longer hours if her partner lost his job, in which case he would stay at home and look after the children.

It is the case in Sweden, however, where the opportunity for paternity leave is very generous, that mothers take 85 per cent of the leave despite the opportunity for fathers to have an equal share.

In Western cultures, family support structures have changed in that families are often living far from the area where they grew up and thus away from grandparents and relatives. Modern technology such as email may keep people in virtual contact but day-to-day practical support is lacking. This means that public child-care arrangements are more necessary. The quality of such care is extremely variable and parents who can afford it turn to private and very expensive arrangements, although these may not necessarily be the best. In other situations the arrangements for looking after children are less than ideal and this is little acknowledged by the Government, which aims to increase the number of parents in the workforce but does not ensure universal, high-quality child care.

We have seen that there are now a number of different family structures, and notions of what constitutes a 'normal' family are challenged, particularly in the inner cities. These family structures include gay parents of both genders, adoptive parents, fathers in second marriages, young fathers and non-resident fathers. For clinical workers these differing and widely varied family structures are a challenge, especially in cities which have multicultural communities.

What are the benefits of father involvement?

Evidence is emerging that a high level of paternal involvement is linked with greater family stability. This may not have been the case so often in the past, as women were very compromised in their roles as wives, often having no earning capacity and thus sometimes having to make the best of a poor marriage. Now that women have a greater role in the workforce, and therefore more financial independence, they do not always have to tolerate partners who do not help with family tasks. However, this has had an effect on family stability.

Many authors state that a high level of father involvement with children produces better outcomes in most areas of child development. Positive effects are in the area of mental and physical health, success at school, and sociability.

Flouri (2005) has researched the outcomes of father involvement. She defines an 'involved' father as one who reads to his children, takes them on outings, is interested in their education, and takes a role equal to that of the mother in managing them. Flouri found that early involvement was positive for later involvement and for good relationships between father and child in adolescence, that children were less likely to be involved with the police, that mental health problems in children were less frequent and that educational attainment was better.

However, Flouri's review of child outcomes (2005) adds to the complexity of the debate. In answer to the question of whether 'good' fathering promotes 'good' child outcomes, she concludes that 'it depends on what we mean by fathering ... what children's outcomes we have in mind and what groups of parents and children we look at' and that 'father involvement was *sometimes* [my italics] associated with "good" outcomes' (p. xii).

In Sweden where parental leave for fathers following childbirth is generous, the higher take-up of this is linked to lower rates of separation and divorce and the more equal sharing of roles in terms of earning and caring (Olah, 2001). These findings are echoed in other research. In my own research (Walters et al., 2001) I found that fathers who had better relationships with their partners were more likely to attend appointments for their child at a Child and Family Psychiatric Service. Snarey (1993) found that fathers were more likely to find happiness in their own marriages if they had histories of involved fathering. Cowan and Cowan (2000) found that the coincidence of beliefs about parenting between parents was important in happy relationships. These aspects are explored further in the Chapter 4.

Cultural aspects of working with fathers

It is a truism to say that the role of fathers varies in different cultures. As practitioners, particularly in multicultural inner-city practices, our job cannot be to understand fully all the myriad beliefs, traditions and roles that come with any family that we see, although we can and must try. Increasingly we are seeing families of mixed race with several cultures within one family which means that we are working with unique situations, somewhat akin to driving without a road map. The challenge as therapists is again to be curious and to elicit the points of view of all the members of the family in order to try and understand their beliefs and stories.

We can only do this through careful questioning, listening and dialogue and being aware of how our own beliefs and traditions filter the information we are receiving. The same applies to class differences, the importance of which is now often underrecognised in favour of an emphasis on culture. Many workers in services have clients from a variety of backgrounds who may not only be from an ethnic minority but may also be unemployed, in council housing, have children in failing schools, and so on.

In addition, although we can look at the literature and learn from it about roles, traditions in other cultures, and so on, cultures are not homogeneous and each family that we see clinically is unique and has its own set of stories and experiences. Being from the Caribbean and being first-generation in the UK, for example, is different from being second-generation. Yet those born here of that generation will still have different histories from a white child born in the UK at the same time. We know from research on families whose forebears were in the Holocaust that trauma can be carried through the generations in subtle ways. Many of the families we see have been more recently traumatised, and many have sought asylum here. They may be clinging to the values of a culture that is not necessarily functional in the UK, and yet the children are having to attend school and carry two cultures, which creates a conflict for them.

A teenage girl whose family had come to the UK from Turkey four years earlier presented, having taken a serious overdose. Her family had very traditional values about how to behave regarding boyfriends, smoking, going out, and so on. These clashes between parents and adolescents can be seen in any family but in this family expectations of behaviour were high. This girl was challenging boundaries more than her siblings, having been influenced by an older girl she had met at school. Her father and elder brother, both educated in Turkey, were particularly punitive towards her for staying out overnight without notice, smoking and drinking. She felt great conflict with the result that she self-harmed. Although the family were offered help the parents were not willing to take this up. Perhaps they feared that the therapy team would side with their daughter?

Further, although a concept of mental illness may be accepted in most cultures, the boundaries between the mental, the psychological and the spiritual may be hard to define. The idea of mental illness can carry great stigma, further creating difficulties for engaging families in services.

Agim was 6 when his father was viciously attacked in his home in Albania by rebel militants. He witnessed the attack from which his father never fully recovered. The family fled overland to the UK with four children. They arrived speaking no English. Agim was the oldest boy. He suffered terrible nightmares several years on. His mother was extremely depressed and Agim as a young child had to take a paternal role (supporting his mother, looking after the younger children, going to the shops, taking his father out) despite being ill-equipped to do so. He went to a failing school and struggled with the language, with disruptive classes, with lack of recognition of his specific learning difficulties. He went home in the evenings and had many chores to fulfil. Through long-term therapeutic work he began to construct a new story of his ordeal when his father was attacked, recognising that he was too young to have made any difference to the attack rather than feeling a failure at not helping his father. He also began to see his father as having been brave rather than helpless. He left school with some qualifications and began training as a carpenter. The family received asylum and were permanently housed after many stressful moves.

Migration to other cultures is usually extremely stressful for families and may mean a change of role for the fathers.

Ahmet's family had moved without their father from another European country where the father remained as he had a good job. His mother found work in the UK. The belief was that the education was better in the UK and that the children would gain more qualifications. Eventually the father joined the family as it was unsatisfactory for him to be abroad alone. He came to the UK speaking little English and could not find work. His role was to look after the three children. For this he had no model or experience, although he seemed a kind and warm man who loved his children. However, his expectations of himself as a provider were crushed and he found himself becoming depressed. The housing was poor, his wife was feeling very stressed in her role as the sole provider and the education in the inner city was extremely disappointing. The family encouraged the father to learn English and this helped him to get a job and also to help his children at home with their education.

There are often different values with regard to how children should behave. These beliefs can be deeply entrenched and require careful exploration. There is sometimes a fine line between what is acceptable and what might constitute child protection. These decisions must be made carefully and with respect for the family's values. Fathers may have a lifetime of beliefs about how their children should be treated based on how they were treated in another culture and these beliefs can be hard to change.

Kefilwe's family had moved from an African country. Kefilwe was seven and one of two children. He was having a lot of problems at school. The teachers suspected physical chastisement at home from his father. In interviews at school which the father attended, the mother sat with her head bowed. To me this looked submissive and my instincts to protect her were aroused. The teacher, however, told me that this was the expected behaviour of women from her culture. The father admitted to hitting his son but was adamant that it was necessary. He saw my assertion that Social Services would need to be informed as interfering but still maintained that he was right and that this is what should happen if his son did not behave. He had most certainly been brought up in this way, having been hit by his own father, and he saw the rules in the UK as a cause of the problems with young people. However, his wife had been to parenting classes in the UK and had adopted the idea of a 'thinking chair' rather than hitting, although these techniques made her feel more isolated from her husband.

It is often helpful when working with families, especially those with complex relationships and histories, to use a genogram to elucidate some of the patterns and to clarify relationships. This can be very engaging for all family members and emphasises the paternal and maternal sides of the family. It can be a particularly useful way of engaging fathers if they are present and can lead to conversations that might otherwise have been more difficult to initiate. Maps are also a useful way of engaging families and fathers when trying to look at stories of migration.

There are examples of cultures in which fathers play a more peripheral role, although it needs to be recognised that non-resident fathers are not always uninvolved with their children. Roopnarine (2004) notes the varying ways in which African- American fathers, despite many not being resident with their children, perceive and carry out their fathering roles, citing educational and economic circumstances as important factors in the variance. As Lamb (2004, p. 19) states, 'Traditional beliefs about male dominance and early sexuality as markers of manhood in African Caribbean communities combine with limited economic opportunities to impede men's participation in children's lives and to place children at increased risk of academic and social difficulties.'

Winston, aged six, had a mother who was mixed race Afro-Caribbean and white British. His father was Afro-Caribbean and left after a period of violence when Winston was 4. Winston had only intermittent contact with his father but held on to the view that he wanted to see him. He was referred for anger problems.

This father fitted the pattern of being unemployed, using drugs and getting involved in criminal activity, which hindered him from fulfilling a parenting role. Father involvement, which can be high among African-American fathers even when non-resident, drops off dramatically as the children get older. For those involved in crime and drugs this is probably more true. They are also often victims of stereotyping and therefore seen by services as being very difficult to help.

I was impressed by the attitude at a conference of a black youth-support worker who had grown up in south London and who said that he and most of his friends had had absent fathers and that they had grown up not really being unhappy with the situation.

'My mum took care of us. I don't think it's affected me that much. I'm not the only one in the world.'

But Cosby and Pouissant, in their book *Come on People* (2007), talk of how this situation of generations of boys growing up without their fathers is really unacceptable. In a stirring text they urge a greater sense of community. The authors analyse the difficulties for black men in the US in gaining employment. But they take a strong line on the responsibilities of fatherhood: 'If you haven't claimed your children, you are not a man' (p. 27). 'Gangs don't raise your children. And to all of you here, we have got to become fathers in our neighbourhoods, fathers to our children, and fathers to every child in that neighbour-hood. We have to understand that we have to be there; the children are only getting 50% because only the mother is there' (pp. 17–18). They go on to say that young men often simply do not know or understand what a father's responsibilities are: 'Many of them have never seen a real father in action. Many do not appreciate that fathers are important to a child's healthy development or that unemployed, separated, and unwed fathers can still interact with their children and contribute significantly to their well-being' (p. 17).

A Nigerian father had grown up in Nigeria where his father had three wives. He saw his father every day.

Another father born in the Gambia was brought up more by his father than his mother after the divorce of his parents. He himself has two children in the Gambia and sees himself as a good father in his role as a provider for them. He also has a child where he lives in the UK but does not live with the mother.

Cabrera and Coll (2004) and Lamb (2004) studied Latino fathers and note that the situation is very complex, with diverse social, cultural and economic histories and patterns of immigration. This limits generalisations. In addition, there is little research. Cabrera and Coll show, however, that the research findings in the 1990s for this group were different from those in the 1960s and 1980s. Women's participa-tion in the workforce has changed fathering practice so that, as with Anglo-American and UK families, there has been a more egalitarian picture in middle-class families. However, research populations are small, further limiting generalisations.

O'Brien (2004) highlights the situation in Europe where father-hood is being redefined in the light of such changes as those in fam-ily structures and in patterns of fertility, employment and migration. Legislation such as that in relation to paternity leave is also altering patterns of fathering. In addition, fathers may be less permanent in children's lives and children may have stepfathers or other role models. It is not known how this will impact on future generations and patterns of fathering.

Barry's parents split when he was six. He said he felt ' a bit insecure, a lot of my friends had dads' and went on to say how he did not believe in marriage. He was somewhat ambivalently separated from his partner but saw his son daily.

Johan had never had any contact with his father and found when he was young that he envied other children. At around the age of nine, however, he said that that changed as he became aware that not all fathers were 'ideal'.

Emil was embarrassed at the age of 14 when his parents split. He rationalised that it was 'for the best'. He now feels, however, that he wants to be the exact opposite of his own father.

Japanese, Chinese and Korean cultures are written about by Shwalb et al. (2004). In these cultures fathers spend less time with their children. Fathers' occupations impact on their roles in a similar way to in the West. Crystal (1994) reviewed the role of the father in Japanese culture, where fathers are found to have more emotional distance from their children than in some cultures. Crystal felt that concomitantly the mother turns more to the child for intimacy and companionship than might be the case in other cultures.

Fu Keung Wong et al. (2003) write of the stresses that come with increased parental involvement in families in Hong Kong. They studied 131 fathers with children aged 2–12. They found that poorer mental health occurred in fathers who perceived their children as being more problematic. A measure of self-efficacy was used and the study showed that those fathers who perceived themselves as being able to deal with their children's difficulties were less stressed and had better mental health. This paper is interesting in explaining the rationale for a more authoritarian style of fathering based on traditional Confucian beliefs. Children are trained to be obedient, and to 'exercise self-control and to accept social obligations' (p. 104). Fathers are considered inadequate if they are not disciplinarian.

Of those fathers who live in non-industrial communities, patterns again differ as Hewlett (2004), who compares industrial and forager societies, points out. Men grow up in closer contact with children in these societies, whereas in industrial societies men are more likely to learn about children when they have their own. Men are less involved in societies where warfare is more common. This is interesting as since World War Two there has been an increase in paternal involvement and National Service has been abandoned. Perhaps men are more able to afford emotional contact with their children when they are not in a situation where they may be called up to fight and be killed and it is safer to keep emotional distance.

Where I work in Hackney there are many different ethnic groups and it is necessary to be flexible in approach. In the Orthodox Jewish community, for example, roles are traditional. Fathers often do not come to clinic appointments where the workers are non-Jewish as they are not allowed to make eye contact or shake hands with non-Jewish women.

Hackney has a substantial Muslim population. In the UK as a whole they are more likely to marry young, to be unemployed, to work unsocial hours and to have no qualifications. The families are also larger than average and have high rates of ill health. Accommodation is often crowded. This means that the fathers in Muslim families are often young and are more absent if employed because of the type of employment. Muslim fathers are often the disciplinarians in the family. Teen relationships with fathers can be difficult, especially if the foundations of the relationships when the children were young were poor. Talking about sexuality, which can be seen as a taboo subject, is often difficult.

In a fathers' group, Arif talked about sexuality and dealing with a daughter in puberty on his own. Arif who is from Pakistan had split up with his wife. At the point where the children were about to be taken into care, he decided to look after them himself. He talked with the group about how difficult it was as a lone father to bring up a teenage daughter. There were no other figures, such as aunts or female adult friends, to whom she could turn, and Arif was finding the situation very isolating. Another man from the group told of his widowed brother who was experiencing a similar situation, although there were cultural differences. Arif seemed reassured to hear this story and to have shared his dilemmas.

Flouri (2005) carried out a study on psychological adjustment in 360 white British and 222 Indian children. All lived with two biological parents and were at the same secondary school in southern England. The girls from both groups showed similar levels of adjustment and similar levels of father involvement. However, lower total difficulties scores and higher prosocial scores were reported among the Indian boys than among the white boys. The Indian boys also reported higher paternal involvement. Father involvement was, therefore, positively associated with prosocial behaviour in both genders in both ethnic groups. Among the white British boys, lower father involvement was linked to peer problems for the sons and among the girls was linked to both behaviour and peer problems.

A project in Bradford set up to involve parents in their children's education found that Asian fathers have additional barriers such as language problems, long, unsocial working hours, the need to support elderly relatives in Pakistan, and problems with mixing with unrelated men and women. These factors mitigate their ability to be involved in the education and upbringing of children. The fathers expressed their desire to be more involved and to have a separate venue and a male worker (Razwan, 2006).

It has been stated by Kraemer (2000) that males are more vulnerable from the beginning of life: 'Where caregivers assume that from birth a boy ought to be tougher than a girl his inborn disadvantage will be amplified' (p. 1611). He continues to say that where males are more highly valued, as in Bangladesh, 'they get relatively better care, probably because girls are neglected'. It is noticeable how, when working with Bengali families, it is often the father who will bring the children to appointments as he is the one who speaks English. In these situations it is important to have an interpreter.

It is always essential to have an interpreter where one or both parents do not speak sufficiently good English. It is tempting to allow, for example, an older child to interpret but this is not always best practice as it puts pressure on that child who may not wish to act in that role. Working with an interpreter can be slower and, to me anyway, can feel more concrete. However, the slower pace can be advantageous in terms of giving the worker time to think carefully as the meeting progresses. It is very important to have an interpreter who sticks to the role of interpreting and does not distort the sense of what is being said. I have had experiences of interpreters who wish to put their own therapeutic stance on the material and this can be a hindrance. However, one can also learn a lot from good interpreters about cultural norms. Keeping the same interpreter is very important for longer-term work, although resources do not always allow this. It is also very important that the interpreter be accurately matched to the client's particular culture as there may be a clash of idiosyncratic beliefs if this is not the case. For example, if I were in the situation of needing an interpreter in another country and culture, I might find it difficult to have an interpreter from another part of my home country of a different age or social class, despite the common language.

The quality of the interpreter should supersede his or her gender but I do think that if a father is the one who needs an interpreter, it may well be worth trying to find a male. Often people working with families are female and another man in the room could be helpful and encouraging for a father.

Mehmet, aged 13, was referred for depression and falling behind in his school work. He was struggling academically and was acting up at home, being rude and abusive towards his mother. His mother, who was bringing up five children without any support from either them or her husband, was also depressed. Her husband worked nights and, according to Mehmet, was 'always sleeping'.

For the first appointment only mother and son attended, despite me asking for both parents to attend. The mother said she would rather her husband did not attend. I asked if this was all right with him and she, of course, told me that it was. After the first appointment I stressed the importance of the father coming to meet me and asked to meet with the parents alone. The father did not speak much English and I offered for them to have an interpreter. I was able to speak to the father on the telephone to ensure that he attended the appointment.

Mehmet's father told me of his upbringing in Turkey which had been very strict, although in a rural setting and so without the restrictions and threats of the inner-city environment experienced by his sons and daughters. He had a father who was not always in work but also did not share domestic tasks and so he grew up with very traditional role models. Clearly he believed that his role was to bring in the money while his wife 'kept house' and looked after the children. I raised the issue of his wife actually wanting to go out to work and he and his children perhaps sharing more of the tasks but he was not in favour of this. I could see that his wife felt that the conversation would not lead anywhere and that she would not want me to pursue this. However, it emerged that when he had had a day job he had been able to spend more time at weekends with the children. Now that he worked nights that situation seemed to have changed. He said that he tried to talk with his son about school and behaviour and about how if it were him he would work harder but he just felt that he could not influence his son if he were not prepared to do this.

The situation was somewhat resolved by a change of school. For the moment this family did not want to look at more entrenched role issues and I felt sure that I should respect this.

Conclusion

There have been many changes in paternal involvement over the last 50 years. Some of this is due to the economic situation and to the changing roles of women who are more frequently employed outside the home. Ironically this has probably contributed to the rise of single-parent households, headed in the majority by women. Women's expectations of men's involvement in family life have changed, with more women expecting and wanting men to take more of the child-care role. The proliferation of interest in fathers is a result of this, creating a greater awareness of the potential for father involvement in family life and the importance of this for children's development. As clinicians we need to be cognisant of the changes in family structures and the meanings and beliefs of families within this and in a variety of cultural groups in order to work as constructively as possible.

Practice points

- It is obvious that fathers' roles vary in different cultures and in and to explore the beliefs and traditions surrounding the roles of mothers and fathers in the families we work with and to acknowledge the heterogeneity within cultures and classes.
- Consider how clients' beliefs and traditions surrounding family may differ from your own. How might this affect your practice? Should it?
- Doing a genogram with the family can be very revealing of roles and relationships down the generations and help some families to look at patterns in a way that may be easier than just talking.
- It is essential regularly to discuss clinical work from a social and cultural perspective, and many services have active workshops for this purpose. Sustaining a dialogue with colleagues about these issues and sharing ideas can be extremely helpful.

2

THE ROLE OF THE FATHER

Inevitably the role of the father has changed throughout history and is closely linked to economic structures in societies. We have moved from the cavemen in hunter-gatherer societies where gender roles were very distinct through to the twentieth and twenty-first century's 'new man' in Western societies where gender roles are often more blurred. The role of the father has changed and is still changing in the Western world from that of provider to a more nurturing role. Kraemer (1993) discusses how in pre-agricultural and primate societies the father's role was mainly that of conception. Men needed to be supreme because of the threat and envy of women. The role of women has changed from that of an unpaid or low-paid part of the economic workforce, dependent on men for their economic survival. In some parts of the West they have now gained independence in their own right – they able to earn their own money and to make choices about having children. However, we frequently have stark public reminders of the contradictions in the roles for men – some men are going to war and being killed. Although this has always happened, it stands out more obviously in a climate where men's nurturing role is being encouraged.

Moloney (2002) reflects on the roles of men and fathers in his paper, 'Coming out of the Shed'. He uses the shed, stuck at the end of the garden and a male preserve, as a metaphor for masculinity. 'They are a continuing symbol of men's orientation to the world outside, whereby they contribute resources to the family but take time and energy away from relationships with partners and children' (p. 71). He dissects entrenched attitudes about women being the nurturers of relationships within the family and men being oriented to the outer world and a providing role. Moloney sees men's self-worth as accordingly entwined with their perceived success in the workplace: 'Love and intimacy are not privileged as major areas of competency for men' (p. 69). Moloney also sees family courts as ratifying this view. Through a moving story of his own family over three generations, Moloney illustrates the difficulties that men have in being allowed to recognise and express emotions when they have been made to go to war and to be the main provider in the family. With changes in these patterns, however, men still struggle to alter the stereotypes by which they are characterised. Moloney makes some salient points about working therapeutically with men and recognising our own images of men and how these may affect the therapeutic context (see Chapter 5).

It is often useful to go back to earlier research, and that of John and Elizabeth Newson (1963) provides us with invaluable studies of urban childcare and the role of fathers in the 1950s in Nottingham (UK). Their research was done in pre-computer days and I remember Elizabeth telling me how they used to thread data cards on knitting needles to count up percentages! We learn from other texts (Hoggart, 1957; Young and Wilmott, 1957) that father-hood has doubtless always been important but socially constructed as secondary to images of masculinity. Even in the 1950s Young and Willmott's study in the East End of London cited the reduction of the working week as being important in allowing fathers to spend more time with their children: 'Nowadays the father as well as the mother takes a hand in the care of the children. It used to be thought very undignified for men to have anything to do with children. You'd never see a man wheeling a pram or holding a baby. Of course that's all changing now' (p. 28).

Despite the popular conception that fathers in the past have not been very involved in the domestic arena, there is little hard data on this. The Newsons' (1963, 1968) study, a longitudinal study of 700 families in the 1950s and 1960s, collected data on paternal involve-ment in the home and found, for example, that in this working-class community 30 per cent of fathers regularly put their one-year-old children to bed and 83 per cent played with their child 'often'. In their study of four- year-olds, the Newsons reported the high partic-ipation of fathers in their children's care in half their sample, with a trend towards the fathers of higher social class being more participa-tive. These examples are interesting in that the popular conceptions of fatherhood in those days was of less rather than more involve-ment with their children. In fact in the 1950s the predominant theory of parenting was driven by Bowlby's ideas on the prime importance of the mother as a parent. These ideas were in the context of a post-war economy where women, having been out at work and hugely important in the workforce when men were away fighting, had been relegated back to the home. The involvement of fathers at that time was more hidden; it is now far more common to see fathers at the school gates or pushing a buggy in the park.

Lummis (1982) has documented an historical analysis of fathering in the early 1900s in East Anglia (UK) from interviews with fishermen and their families. Lummis studies three categories of fishermen – driftermen away from home for up to twenty weeks at a time, but with four months at home not working; trawlermen who were away four or five nights a week on a regular basis; and inshoremen who worked ordinary hours and were home daily. Also included were men who were not fishermen and worked in other manual jobs. Lummis points out that his data fails to support the stereotypes of fathers in working-class families as brutal and uncaring. He cites quality of evidence as being of crucial importance and careful interviewing reveals a different picture of fathers who contribute to the household in many different ways. There are examples of families seeming to work together to get the chores done with every member, including the children, having a role: 'The performance of fatherhood roles cannot be divorced from socially imposed divisions of labour which have excluded the male from the home as effectively as they have tied women to it' (Lummis, 1982).

Minuchin (1974) writes about the 'nuclear family [being] a recent historical development ... largely confined to urban industrialised societies' and goes on to say that 'until four hundred years ago was not seen as a child-rearing unit, and not until much later were children recognised as individuals in their own right' (p. 49). The history of childhood as a concept is beautifully written about by Aries (1962).

Feminist writers more radically opine that 'there is no social, psychological or developmental justification to legislate for father presence' (Perlesz, 2005, p. 22). Perlesz sees 'father absence fear' as 'a pretext to regain the hegemony of patriarchal nuclear family life' and to encourage the power and control of men in families as a right. Perlesz writes from the role of a lesbian parent but interestingly, having raised her daughter with her partner, tells of how her daughter values her biological and social connection with her father. Perlesz quotes Silverstein and Auerbach (1999), who state that children require 'at least one responsible, caretaking adult who has a positive emotional connection to them and with whom they have a consistent relationship'. They feel that neither a father nor a mother is essential for this. Some, however, would disagree and hold the view that fathers do have a specific role, particularly with sons. This is examined more fully in the section below on research findings on fathers and gender of child.

What is fathering?

What is fathering? Clearly there is no single concept of fathering – it is a constantly evolving role and differs widely according to class and culture. There are differing theoretical views on fathering roles according to the various academic schools. I will not attempt to describe these in detail here, although a brief mention of the differ-ent models is necessary.

The development of psychoanalytic theories with regard to fathers are written about in detail by Etchegoyen and Trowell (2002). It is interesting to think about how much importance was placed on the role of the father in these theories, which were quite patrocentric at the beginning of the twentieth century. Etchegoyen maps the move from this patrocentricity to more of an emphasis on mothers and the importance of mothering following the Second World War, par-ticularly in the works of Klein, Anna Freud and Mahler, and later in the works of Bowlby, Winnicott and Bion. Lacan agreed with Freud about the importance of the Oedipus complex and for a description of his theories and their relation to fathers, see an excellent and suc-cinct piece by Featherstone (2009).

Skynner (1976) moved from working psychodynamically and often with mother–child dyads to becoming interested in working with the wider family. He is well known in his intervention with children who are phobic about attending school for having insisted on the father becoming involved in taking the child to school. In my clinical experience this view still has some credence. Skynner talks of the need for the father to play a role in which he assists with the separation of the child from its mother. He sees the father as a boundary-keeper, holding the view that the child's life begins 'within the mother': 'The child has to move away from its initial attachment to the mother towards a greater involvement with the outside world, and in this the father is situated in an intermediate position, a bridge between the two worlds' (1976, p. 147). However, Skynner goes on to say that either gender can in fact manage both boundaries and that where mothers are raising children alone this can be accomplished by them filling both roles. Dowling and Gorrell Barnes (2000) talk of how in post-divorce arrangements in the 1990s fathers are able to 'take on patterns of parenting which include doing jobs formerly defined as belonging to women, or more usually seen culturally within the domain of "mothering"' (p. 19). Ultimately Skynner talks of the complementarity of the roles of mother and father which changes throughout the life cycle. To return to the school-phobic child, Skynner talks of 'the inability of the father to fulfil his paternal role' (p. 308) and refers to weakness and dependence.

There is no doubt that times have changed since Skynner wrote in the 1970s and that family structures are more diverse. Women's employment outside the home has increased and there is greater state support for families where the father is absent. Clinicians in inner cities are working with a wide range of ethnic groups and family constellations. Some of the ideas around fathers' roles with which Skynner worked would be less easily applied or even accepted by today's clinicians. However, they still have a powerful resonance and provide an interesting part of the historical journey from psychodynamic theory through to systemic theory and the development of ways of working with families.

The role of fathers in children's development is amply explored by several authors but most notably Lamb (2004). His book explores father involvement and its nature, fathers' influences on children, determinants of father involvement, and policy applications. Importantly, the overall conclusions are that 'fathers and mothers influence their children in similar rather than dissimilar ways' (p. 10). 'Paternal warmth, nurturance, and closeness are associated with positive child outcomes regardless of whether the parent involved is a mother or a father. The important dimensions of parental influence are those that have to do with parental characteristics rather than gender-related characteristics' (p. 10). He continues to state that the characteristics of individual fathers are less important than the *relationships* that they have with their children (my italics). He emphasises relationships that are 'secure, supportive, reciprocal, and sensitive'. In the same vein, the amount of time spent with children is less important than what is done in that time and the perceptions by all parties of that relationship and its meaning. Lamb also emphasises the importance of family context and harmony in parental relationships. Fathers also need to feel competent and fulfilled in themselves.

Despite individual studies showing varying outcomes, Lamb finally states, 'There is no single father's role to which all fathers should aspire. Rather, a successful father, as defined in terms of his children's development, is one whose role performance matches the demands and prescriptions of his sociocultural and familial context. This means that high paternal involvement may have positive effects in some circumstances and negative in others. The same is true of low paternal involvement' (p. 11).

Attachment theory originated with John Bowlby's work in 1969 and was linked with psychodynamic theories of child development. Essentially, mothers were seen as the key attachment figure for the infant, and research was based around this. However, Bowlby did state that a principal attachment figure could be someone other than the mother. The theories were in the context of a post-war economic climate where women were far less commonly at work and stayed at home with their children.

As employment patterns have changed and fathers are more prominent in terms of taking a nurturing role in the family, researchers have begun to look at fathers and attachment, and what relevance this has for child development. This research still feels relatively new although in fact there were studies on father–child attachment in the 1970s and 1980s when there was a particular wave of interest in fatherhood (Lewis, 1982). As early as 1980, Lamb was saying that children may be attached differently to mothers and fathers (secure with one and not the other) and acknowledging the different ways in which parents may relate. Lamb also reported on father–child attachment being related to children's orientation to novel situations.

Father–child attachment is an interesting area and questions are often asked about whether attachment to the mother moulds the fundamental attachment of the child or whether it is a joint effect. Bogels and Phares (2008) posit that father–child attachment may have a particular role in decreasing childhood anxiety in that secure father–infant attachment is more related than mother–infant attachment to the approach to novel social situations and to later peer attachment. Past research has indicated that children can grow up with different attachment models for each parent. However, it is likely that one attachment style will become dominant. Some of the studies quoted by Bogels and Phares in the area of attachment are now quite old and this is clearly an area for current research, given that fathers' roles are changing so much. However, one study quoted (Grossman et al., 2002) found that father–infant sensitive-play attachment was a better predictor of adolescents' secure attachment to peers than early mother–child attachment.

Some studies (Fox et al., 1991) suggest that attachment classification is concordant between mother and father. This might be explained by the idea that parents choose each other according to shared attitudes. However, work by Main (1999) found that early attachment to father was not related to attachment at age 19 but rather attachment to mother. This pertained even in Sweden where fathers stayed at home and mother went out to work. Main suggests that the earliest experiences, including prenatal experiences, start with the mother and this may be relevant.

Lamb (2004) states that quality of father–child attachment is related to peer competence, although research findings are mixed. Overall, however, the research literature remains unclear about father–infant attachment and how children might negotiate the different attachment styles of each parent.

Research findings on fathers and gender of child

Anecdotally we all know examples of what we perceive as 'good' fathering. In many ways the idea of father as provider has shifted, particularly in Western cultures where women are more likely now to be working outside the home and parenting can be more shared between fathers and mothers. The image of a 'good' father is now less one of a provider and more of a contributor, one of someone who is involved in childcare as well as going out to work, a somewhat androgynous role. But what does research tell us about the effects of fathers on sons as opposed to daughters? Eirini Flouri (2005) concludes in her book on fathering and child outcomes that 'father involvement was *sometimes* associated with "good" children's outcomes (e.g. it was positively related to happiness and academic motivation) and *sometimes* unrelated to "good" children's outcomes (e.g. early father involvement was not related to career maturity in adolescence, or to labour-force participation, state benefits receipt and subsidised housing in adult life)' [my italics] (p. 187). She continues to say that 'certain aspects of father involvement in certain groups of fathers was associated with certain outcomes in certain groups of children' and goes on to cite specific examples. These are that father involvement has been found to be associated with low risk for delinquency in sons but not daughters in that there is evidence for links between father involvement and adolescents' externalising behaviours. Flouri and Buchanan (2004) carried out four studies (two cross-sectional and two longitudinal) examining the role of father involvement in the academic outcomes of their children and concluded that interest by fathers in a child's education is shown to be related to adult daughters' but not sons' educational attainment in adult life, and that father involvement protected against an experience of homelessness in adult sons but not daughters from low socio-economic groups.

From my own research (Walters, 1999) it was indicated that where boys are the referred client, the engagement of fathers is particularly important. This is in view of the finding that fathers' reported depressive symptoms were positively correlated with their ratings of the behaviour of their sons but not of their daughters, and that mothers' depressive symptoms were positively correlated with their ratings of the behaviour of their daughters but not of their sons. Furthermore, fathers' depressive symptoms were related to their reports of care from their own fathers but not their mothers. These findings have important implications for clinical work in that although we are often working to encourage father involvement, it may be even more important where boys are the referred clients.

Overall, it is difficult to tease out clear effects from studies: some show the importance of fathers; others are less clear. A number of studies cite evidence of the positive effects of father involvement and differing effects for boys and girls. Sarkadi et al. (2008) carried out a systematic review of longitudinal evidence from 24 publications of the effects of father involvement on children's developmental outcomes. They found evidence that father engagement reduces the frequency of behavioural problems in boys and psychological problems in young women.

A study based on the National Institute of Child Health and Human Development Study of Early Care and Youth Development by Bell and Belsky (2007) found that more supportive parenting during the pre-school years is associated with lower heart rates and blood pressure in primary school children, particularly in relation to fathering and sons. Bronte-Tinkew et al. (2008) looked at father involvement and cognitive development in infants. Aspects of father involvement such as paternal warmth and care-giving activities were shown to be positively associated with less cognitive delay. This was found to be greater in relation to sons and also to infants with disabilities.

A further study (Craigie, 2008) found that in families which are less stable, cognitive outcomes in children are poorer. Thus where the family is single-parent or two-parent, stability is key and statistically similar for both constellations. Where the family is more disruptive and paternal presence is partial, effects on cognitive performance are deleterious and the authors report findings that the effect is greater for girls than boys.

From a large British dataset (Nettle, 2008) it has been shown that paternal involvement in childhood has positive associations with offspring at age 11 and offspring social mobility by age 42. There is an interaction with regard to IQ between the socio-economic status (SES) of the father and his level of involvement in that fathers of higher SES were shown to make more difference to the child's IQ from their investment than were fathers of low SES. The authors state that there was no differential effect on sons' or daughters' mobility, which were the same.

Ramchandani and Psychogiou (2009) suggest that boys are more vulnerable than girls where their fathers are depressed, especially early on in their lives. There is also research suggesting that sons of alcoholic fathers are at risk of developing conduct disorder, delinquency, and substance use. Ramchandani and Psychogiou further suggest that fathers may spend more time with sons than daughters.

Nonetheless, Lamb (2004) points out that the relevance of father involvement with girls and boys has changed as gender roles have become less stereotyped and as a need has arisen for more flexibility with regard to those roles. Research findings over the years reflect these sociocultural changes.

Do families need fathers?

Leon, aged eight, was referred for soiling and wetting. I talked about Leon's feelings about not seeing his father whose whereabouts are unknown. His father turned up when he was four but he has not seen him since. He told me that it feels 'a bit sad' not having a dad around, it would be a 'better family' with a mum and a dad. A mum 'needs someone to help her when she is tired'. A dad could 'help me and my sister do homework, take the children to the park, play football'. He also thought that a father could help to walk the dog and teach him to ride a bike. Leon said that if he were a dad he would stay with his wife and children and not just go away. He said he would become really sad if he were a father who did not see his family again.

The extreme feminist stance on this would be that fathers are not necessary to raise children. The other extreme might be psychoanalytical ideas where theories around the Oedipal complex mean that emotional development cannot be negotiated properly without a father to fulfil this role. However, these are polemic views and there is no simple answer. Most lives are complex and seldom fit neatly into theoretical models, despite what research may tell us. Accounts of case studies are also mediated by the authors and their histories and it is impossible to know a 'truth' on this. The question might be answered by individuals:

A little boy of white British/African-American origin, who was not allowed contact with his father as a result of the father's behaviour with regard to drug use, told me ' I miss my dad but he lies and steals.' This child, despite being very young, was able to hold these two ideas: that of a dad whom he loved and that of a dad who did wrong. He was referred , unsurprisingly, for aggressive outbursts, perhaps indicating the conflict he was trying to contain.

However, on a basic level it is probably easier to bring up children with two parents rather than one, provided that those parents or parental figures have a cooperative relationship. The question of whether one of the parents needs to be a man is more specific. Tasker and Golombok's research (1997) into lesbian parenting found that children of lesbian parents had no more difficulties growing up than children of heterosexual relationships. There was a similar outcome in relation to gay men and parenting (Tasker, 2005; see also Chapter 4). A same-sex couple may be subject to many prejudices. However, the gay couples I have worked with show an enormous commitment to their children's upbringing.

In a paper by Bogels and Phares (2008) the authors ask whether fathers matter in contributing to the development of children. They look at paternal play, attachment, involvement and also at indirect roles in terms of partner support. The authors conclude that there are many benefits to fathers' play with their children. Paternal play 'seems to promote an active, competitive, autonomous, and curi-ous attitude in children, has a beneficial effect on children's social and cognitive development, and seems to buffer early separation, stranger and novelty anxiety' (p. 542). They do, however, comment importantly on the bidirectionality of these effects in that the more playful the father, the more socially competent a child may become, thus increasing the positive involvement of the father.

A striking finding from research (Bogels and Phares, 2008) is that from cross- sectional as well as longitudinal studies the evidence strongly suggests that paternal closeness and involvement more than maternal closeness and involvement 'promotes competence and protects against psychological distress in adolescents and young adults' (p. 543). Interestingly, the authors state that these effects are independent of levels of maternal involvement, divorce or even the gender of the child. However, it is in adolescence and young adulthood that children are more likely to be separated from their fathers, although that does not necessarily mean that his influence and presence is not there. From this research it seems that the need to promote contact and engagement is strong.

Sarkadi et al. (2008) have reported on a systematic review of longitudinal studies on the effects of father involvement on the developmental outcomes in children. They reviewed 24 publications which included biological fathers and father figures. They used a definition of the involvement of fathers which included accessibility, engagement and responsibility. There were a number of positive findings, with evidence to suggest that the active and regular engagement of fathers (direct interaction with the child) was effective in reducing behavioural problems in boys and psychological problems in young women, in enhancing cognitive development and in decreasing delinquency and economic disadvantage. There was also evidence to suggest that the cohabitation of mother and father or mother and male partner results in fewer externalising behaviour difficulties. This review was carried out in order to influence policies promoting fathering which need al. (good evidence to support their introduction. Interestingly, a study by Levy-Schiff et al. (1994) found that a high level of father involvement at age six was associated with more hyperactivity at age fourteen!

However, overall the authors state that there is enough evidence 'to support the intuitive assumption that engaged fathers are good for their children. This seems especially valid when it comes to children at risk of poor outcomes' (Sarkadi et al., 2008, p. 157).

In practical terms the authors urge professionals working with families actively to include fathers in consultations and even to indicate clearly to parents the proven importance of the father's role. Moreover, they state that there is sufficient evidence for policy-makers to improve the circumstances with regard to involved fathering.

Lone fathers

Family structures are changing rapidly and we frequently meet families that are reconstituted with stepfathers and families where there is no father. There is much literature on separated parents but very little on separated fathers who are living with their children. Although they are in the minority, there are nonetheless a substantial number of fathers bringing up children alone and this number is increasing. There is ample scope for research in this area. Although parental separation is very common, we should not minimise the impact that this has on children.

At least one in three children under the age of 16 will experience the separation of their parents (Joseph Rowntree Foundation, 2004) and 30 per cent will experience long-term difficulties, particularly where there is considerable family disruption. Hofferth et al. (2002) state that in the US there are 2.5 per cent of children living with a single father. In the UK there are approximately 6 million single parents, 9 per cent of whom are fathers (Office for National Statistics, 2006). This represents large numbers of fathers bringing up children alone.

'It's hard being a father, it is even harder being a single father' (father in fathers' group).

Gingerbread, a UK organisation for lone parents, reports on a survey in which 115 lone fathers completed a questionnaire. Issues raised by 360 lone father callers to the Gingerbread advice line in 2000 were also monitored. The survey was investigated because of feedback that lone fathers felt 'invisible and that their existence and issues were not being acknowledged or addressed' (Gingerbread, 2000, p. 1). Half of this group of fathers had children of pre-school or primary age. Given that children in families headed by lone fathers tend to be older than children in other types of families, the proportion with younger children may be particularly isolated. Many of the fathers felt not only that they were isolated but also that society had a negative attitude towards them. Employment was a big issue, with 83 per cent being employed prior to lone fatherhood and 20 per cent less than this afterwards. Many had reduced their working hours because of their childcare responsibilities and some found that this had a detrimental effect on their career in much the same way as for women bringing up children. Loss of income was another important factor.

Some fathers found that they needed to develop the new skills of involving themselves in their children's education and healthcare and of cooking and providing food, and 18.5 per cent found caring for girls something that they needed support with or had to learn about. Some lone fathers received support from neighbours or relatives but others felt very isolated and wanted an individual or group to support them. A minority continued to live and parent under considerable stress.

However, 80 per cent felt that their relationship with their children had become closer as a result of conscious attempts at greater communication and involvement.

Gingerbread calls for the parenting role of lone fathers to be recognised and valued in particular by policy-makers, by those delivering services and by employers. Rights to parental paid leave, time off for emergencies and reduced working hours are highlighted.

In our fathers' group meetings at the clinic where I work, we often have fathers who are separated from their partners, frequently as a result of the partners' addictions, and are bringing up children alone. I struggled for some time with my thoughts about how hard it was for women to bring up children alone and to understand why it should be any different for men. I then began to realise that lone fathers have a set of hurdles to overcome that are different from those of lone mothers. They have in many cases been socialised into being breadwinners and then, as lone parents of young children, they find themselves unable to work because they are only free during school hours. They also find it much harder to socialise and network than do women in common settings such as at the school gates and so they find it particularly hard to develop a supportive network. Women who do not work or who work part-time to allow them to bring up children experience no stigma but this is not the case for men.

There is ample evidence that children suffer as a result of serious parental conflict. I have used the word 'serious' as modern parents often feel under great pressure to be 'perfect', never to have arguments and so on, for fear of damaging their children. Arguments are part of normal life and children can learn from conflict and resolution. However, where conflict is persistent and severe and where relationships are unremediable, damage is much more likely, but is mediated by the resilience and temperament of the children, the relationship with each parent, and other factors such as support from the school and the wider family. Many studies show children to suffer behavioural difficulties, depression and anxiety as a result of conflict (Cummings et al., 2004). Many of these children are referred to child services or are noticed at school and brought to the attention of services. Overall, the effects do not seem to be more pronounced for either girls or boys, although individual studies will show otherwise. Physical violence is particularly damaging and children are likely to use this to express anger when they have witnessed it (Jenkins, 2000).

Cassano et al. (2006) cite data showing that in the US in 1960 6 per cent of families were headed by women but that by 2003

68 per cent of children lived with two parents, 23 per cent with their mothers, and 5 per cent with their fathers. Single fathers in the US have increased from 393,000 in 1970 to 2.3 million in 2003. In 2002 one-fifth of dependent children in Britain lived in lone-parent families. Single fathers may be widowed or separated and, in the case of the latter group, this is often because the mother is a substance user and/or has severe mental health problems and the father therefore has care of the children. These situations raise many issues, not least of which is what to tell young children.

Ekrem was forced to separate from the mother of their child as a result of her severe substance use. He struggled with what to tell his young son as he sometimes saw his mother well for brief periods. He found it hard to describe drug addiction to a four-year-old, especially as his mother had periods of being well. The other men in the group helped Ekrem construct a simple narrative for his son using their own experiences.

Narratives do not of course need to be fixed and can change as the child's understanding develops and they question more.

Separated fathers

'Separated fathers' is a term which generally refers to fathers who are separated from their families and are not usually living full-time with their children, although they may have some shared care. A study by Gingerbread (Peacey and Hunt, 2009) of 41 separated parents (27 resident, 14 non-resident) focused on child contact and support needs. This was a qualitative study as part of a larger study of 559 separated parents. Most of the non-resident parents were fathers.

Gingerbread calls for more funding for Contact Centres, support for families where contact is found to be difficult, and plans to encourage more separated parents to make arrangements for their children to spend safe, quality time with their parents. Fathers in particular want advice and support on issues arising from separation.

An important aspect of this study is the finding that the stereotypes of 'deadbeat dads' and 'obstructive mothers' need challenging. The authors state that these images are often based on perceptions of others which might be challenged. 'Obstructive mothers and drop-out dads may be more creatures of popular myth than reality' (p. 164). Blame and misperceptions are important factors. Fathers represent the majority of separated parents who live without their children and the popular image is of them not wanting access to their children. Perceptions of the other parent can become polarised where there is little contact. In the Gingerbread study, where there was no contact one-fifth of non-resident parents thought that this was due to the resident parent being reluctant or uncommitted with regard to contact. In contrast, half of the resident parents held the view that it was a lack of commitment on the part of the non-resident parent or that for various reasons it was a choice. However, the authors state, 'In certain of our in-depth interviews it was easy to envisage how something which the interviewee was putting forward as reasonable behaviour on their part or unreasonable behaviour on the other person's could be seen in quite another way, and had we been able to interview the other parent, very probably would have been' (p. 164). What is clear is that maintaining contact with parents post-separation is often a very difficult task and even those parents who are committed to contact may find it hard at times. Various suggestions are made for facilitating this: access to mediation, quality advice, Family Relationship Centres (as in Australia), counselling services and more pastoral support in schools. As far as schools are concerned, it is important for them to keep both parents in touch regarding correspondence, parents evenings, and so on.

Overall, the study found that although few parents seek court intervention, there are often major issues following separation. Not everyone requires professional help but some do seek this and existing services need to be publicised.

Jayden, aged 11, presented with suicidal thoughts following the separation of his parents. His mother had left for somebody new. Jayden saw his father as being uncommunicative and his mother as the one who organised everything and kept the family going. Now the parental roles were reversed, with the father doing the bulk of the chores in the family home and looking after Jayden and two younger siblings. Jayden was very angry about the changes and worried about how his father would cope. A series of meetings with both parents and Jayden enabled him to voice his fears and to be reassured that in fact his father was competent and could manage. Jayden began to see the evidence of this as his father altered his working hours to accommodate his new responsibilities and also to realise that he too had to change and do more to help in the home. Sessions were arranged with father and son to think about the new household and their relationship.

There is no uniform package of help that can be used in these situations. However, there are certain ideas that can be helpful to many families who find themselves in this situation and these are outlined in Dowling and Gorrell Barnes (2000) who give recommendations following divorce. Important suggestions such as not talking in disparaging ways about the absent parent, usually the father, and caution over the introduction of a new partner are helpful here. Mediation services can also be of great importance where a therapist can be a neutral third party in helping to negotiate through disputes over care and to limit the damage to children. These services can also be key in helping fathers to have a role and to engage with their children in meaningful ways.

Although the overall view is for a positive ongoing relationship with the non-resident parent to be protective, this must not be mis-interpreted as contact in itself being positive. Some contact can be damaging, particularly where there has been abuse or domestic vio-lence. I have learned from working with families and encouraging fathers to attend appointments that in some cases this is not the best approach (see Chapter 5). Dramas can be re-enacted with parents in front of the children that are not helpful and parents may need to be seen separately or without the children.

Mary came to the clinic with her two teenage children whom she was finding difficult to manage. Her daughter in particular was being defiant, coming in late, running up large mobile phone bills, and so on. The father had left the family and was living with his girlfriend and new baby. The children had contact but were often let down. Mary had found this very difficult and was extremely depressed. She was also trying to hold down a job. I decided to invite the father in for a session to discuss the management of the children and to help set some boundaries around contact. I made the mistake, with hindsight, of holding the meeting with the children and both parents. In the session the relationship difficulties were acted out and the children withdrew, seeming to despair at the inevitability of the difficul-ties that the parents had in working together. The father seemed unable to understand the relevance of his behaviour in undermining his ex-partner and disappointing the children. Sessions were therefore tried with just the parental couple although again were not very successful.

Where fathers retain warmth and support, and are involved and authoritative, the outcomes are better for the children (Dunn, 2005). However, a study in the US (Thomas et al., 1996) showed that non-resident father involvement buffered the negative effects of being with a lone mother in terms of child delinquency, heavy drinking and the use of illicit drugs. In the same study, however, the problems of black adolescents were greater when the fathers were involved. It can be the case that where fathers remain involved with their non-resident children the conflict between the parents continues in an explicit way, although this does not explain the cultural differences in this study. Sometimes a child may find it easier to relate to one parent only rather than to sustain relationships with two warring parents. In this case, work with the parents on the importance of not expressing hostile views about the other parent will be helpful.

Children can sometimes experience periods when the father has more contact. Some fathers prefer, for example, to be with their adolescent children than with pre-schoolers. At adolescence children are freer to develop their own relationships with their fathers. Mothers who have blocked contact may have less power to do so at this later stage.

When thinking about the roles fathers play we can learn much from what happens where fathers are absent. Dunn (2004) writes extensively about non-resident fathers. An increasing number of fathers do not live in the same household as their children. Dunn's paper examines such aspects as economic support, frequency of contact and the quality of the relationship between father and child.

Economic support from non-resident fathers is a key factor in children's well-being but is linked to frequency of contact, making a more complex picture. In addition, economic support for mothers is a key factor in their ability to manage their families alone. Young fathers and fathers in general who have a low income or who are unemployed have more difficulty providing financial support and have less contact. Housing is an issue for young and economically compromised fathers as many are not able to provide accommodation for their children, thus making contact more difficult.

Patterns of contact are changing and there is some evidence that children and their non-resident fathers may be seeing each other more frequently. Some research suggests that contact with fathers is positive for children's academic success. However, methodologically Dunn points out that if children are doing well it may encourage more contact, and vice versa. It is suggested by Amato and Gilbreth (1999) that more recent cohorts of fathers studied regarding contact and the well-being of the children may include fathers who are more committed to their parenting role.

Of great importance are the personality and behavioural patterns of the father and there are more likely to be problems among young, unmarried, non-resident fathers than married, resident fathers. A study by Jaffee et al. (2003) on UK twins aged five showed that fathers who engaged in high levels of antisocial behaviour had children who had worse behaviour problems where the father was resident. Where very antisocial fathers did not live with their children, the figures for the children's antisocial behaviour were lower. Where there were low levels of antisocial behaviour and the fathers were non-resident, the figures for children's antisocial behaviour were minimal. This study suggests a strong link between genetics and behaviour and is one of the few studies addressing this, although it is a very important aspect.

It is common for children to want contact with their non-resident father. Where there is resistance the reasons are linked to the unreliability of the contact arrangements, the fathers' distress regarding the contact arrangements, the feeling of being caught in the middle of parental conflict, divided loyalties, the parents' new partners and half-siblings and stepsiblings.

Joe was 16 and had dropped out of school. His father had left some years earlier and Joe had intermittent contact which was not on a regular basis.

Joe's mother had a partner who had moved in two years previously. Around this time Joe began to have angry outbursts, particularly towards his mother, and started truanting from school and staying out at night. His mother was beside herself with anxiety at these times. Joe was referred for help with his family. However, he indicated that he wanted to talk alone. He revealed that he felt that his father did not love him and that this made him feel extremely sad and angry. Since his mother's new partner had moved in he felt even more alone. An older brother had left home the previous year.

With Joe's permission his father was invited to sessions. He attended once but did not follow up with subsequent appointments. He was clearly depressed and did not want to explore this but listened to Joe when he described how alone he felt at home. He started to be more reliable in his contact with Joe and to encourage him to get back to college.

Joe was also able to talk with his mother more about how he felt and she too began to make more time for him. Joe returned to college although spent more time staying at friends' houses. However, he did not disappear without letting his mother know where he was, as he had done previously, and sometimes he stayed the night at his father's.

Contact with non-resident fathers is often unreliable and a source of great turmoil in the children. The emphasis in clinical work is to point out how important regular and reliable contact is in building trust and enabling children to see their parents as people on whom they can depend, even if they do not live with them.

In terms of parenting and the quality of relationships, poor outcome is associated with such variables as hostility and authoritarian parenting, and these apply whether the father is resident or not. This seems to pertain for white, single-mother families studied in the US (Thomas, Farrell and Barnes, 1996) and the UK (Dunn, 2003). However in black, single-mother families, where the children were male adolescents, fewer problems were found when non-resident fathers were NOT involved. Issues raised were family networks, support and the history of the father–child relationship, the mother–child relationship and the parental relationship.

Dunn (2003) talks of 'gate-keeping' by mothers in terms of the children's contact with their fathers. This can involve persistent denigration of the absent parent. This is particularly important when working with families where the father is separated in the sense that one should always communicate with the father directly than through the mother (see Chapter 5). Dunn notes that 'children's opportunity to communicate with both sets of parents about issues that trouble them remains important' (p. 663). Dunn also reports that where fathers have new families they do not see their own children less, although this tends to be mediated by the number of new biological children in the new household.

Where domestic violence has been witnessed, there are often mixed responses from the children in relation to contact with their fathers. There can be relief at the separation by the child, although Dunn cautions that children should still have a right to maintain contact if they wish to do so.

Eric, aged 12, referred for aggression at school, did not wish to have contact with his father, despite encouragement from his mother. This was because he recalled the violence and wanted no reminders of it. His mother had had two marriages, both of which had ended in violence.

Children and parents often say that they see more of their fathers after separation. Fathers may be more relaxed, prefer having confined times to see their children and also feel better about seeing their children without their partner. There is little research on this aspect. Some fathers lose out on the more intimate side of parenting when they are non-resident (e.g. bathtime, bedtime, etc.) but others may develop different ways of being with their children. It may be that fathers can feel more competent as a parent when not in the presence of a partner whom they perceive as critical. There is some evidence (Dunn, 2003, p. 664) that better pre-separation relationships result in better post-separation relationships. However, some parents who were strongly attached become disengaged (Kruk, 1991), probably because it feels too painful for them. Clearly the circumstances of the separation and what happens afterwards are influential factors. Housing, or having somewhere where children can stay, is an important factor. In addition, anything that may influence a father's self esteem, such as suitable employment and good supportive social networks, make a big difference.

In the US White and Gilbreth (2001) report that two-thirds of children with non-resident fathers also have a stepfather. The evidence is equivocal: 'Having a good, supportive relationship with a non-custodial father is linked to good adjustment outcome, and so too is a good relationship with a stepfather. A warm, close relationship with either father-figure is associated with adjustment' Dunn (2003, p. 665). Over time, however, relationships with stepfathers seem to become more important in terms of adjustment. Dunn notes that these findings illustrate the need for longitudinal studies.

What do fathers think about contact? Bradshaw et al. (1999) in a UK study found that ex-partners obstructing access was the reason most often given by non- resident fathers for lack of contact with their children (see above). Other factors that were important were employment and finance, with those fathers who were employed having greater contact. Housing was also an important factor, as was a new partner in the father's life who might create problems.

Ben, aged ten, was an anxious only child whose mother sought help as he insisted on sleeping in her bed. His parents were separated. His father insisted that he had no problem when Ben was staying with him. The mother said that when Ben came back from the father's he looked exhausted and she knew that he had not slept well. Ben was frightened to disturb his father as the father had a new partner.

Some research by Simpson et al. (1995) demonstrated how having a disciplinary role was difficult for non-resident fathers, who often viewed their children as friends rather than describing the role in parent–child terms. If contact with one's children is time-limited, it may feel difficult to set firm boundaries on behaviour for fear of alienating the children. These aspects can be examined when working with parents who are separated.

Interestingly, it is reported by Stewart, Manning and Smock (2003) that non- resident fathers who have more contact with their children are more likely to have new relationships. This may be the result of personality variables whereby fathers who are able to be warm and nurturing with their children are also more capable of adult partnerships.

Variables such as the age of the child at separation, the duration of time since separation and the stability of the arrangements all, over time, affect the outcome measures. In terms of gender the results are equivocal. One study in the US and New Zealand found that father absence was associated with increased sexual activity in girls (Ellis et al., 2003). However, Dunn (2003) comments on the methodology where studies use interviews and self-report from fathers but rarely observation. When studying non-resident fathers it is easier to find those still in contact, which introduces a sampling bias.

Smyth and Moloney (2008) have written a review of the changes in patterns of post-separation parenting over time in Australia and question the notion of 'stability' which may not always be beneficial to children: 'Stability of traditional arrangements (typically residence with one parent, and one or two overnight stays per fortnight or week with the other) suggests a range of assumptions about parenting and children's needs that have been increasingly challenged. But for children, stability of arrangements in which one parent (most frequently the father) is fully or significantly absent is likely to be a more serious issue' (p. 19). Smyth and Moloney suggest how disengagement by fathers might reflect a number of situations such as 'alienation' by the main caretaking parent as a way of resolving conflict where the situation is too painful. Where there has been pre-separation violence, abuse, neglect or indifference, the 'continued involvement of both parents after separation is a goal not always worthy of unequivocal or universal support' (p. 19). The authors further warn about being 'rigid or formulaic' with families in transition and point out that arrangements will need to change over time to suit the needs of the family and the ages of the children. However, fluidity of arrangements can also reflect family chaos and should be taken into account.

Stepfathers

There is a considerable body of work on stepfathers, who can, like biological fathers, present risks and resources in children's lives. Dunn (2004) states that the impact of stepfathers on self-esteem can be very powerful. Stepfathers can have highly influential effects on children's adjustment, depending on the duration of the remarriage (Hetherington, 1993). However, Radhakrishna et al. (2001) found that stepfather–child relationships are more challenging than biological relationships: they are not as close, stepfathers are less affectionate and more coercive, and stepchildren are less warm and affectionate with stepfathers. Where stepfathers enter children's lives when they are young, adjustment is often better. When the children are older, however, daughters can be particularly resistant to the relationship.

Sarkadi et al. (2008) say that more studies are required to explore the role of biological bonds. There are results which indicate that although non-biological father figures can play an important role for children in their households, biological fathers may be 'salient in a specific way' (Sarkadi et al., 2008, p 157).

Sexual abuse is more likely where fathers are not biological (Radhakrishna et al., 2001) and this is an important factor to bear in mind when working with families. Fathers who are physically close to their children are less likely than stepfathers to be abusers or reported for abuse.

On the whole it is found that children in families with stepfathers do not do better than those in lone-parent families (McLanahan et al., 2006). It is clear that support is needed for men who are step-fathers. Children's behaviour can affect and threaten step-parenting relationships and careful work with family systems may be helpful.

Fathers' relationships with their partners are clearly also a crucial factor and a mediating effect on children's development. Good supportive relationships make for less stress in relation to child-rearing. The implications of this for clinical work are obvious and where parents are not cooperating this will be reflected in the children's behaviour. Helping parents work together and reaching common understandings of children's needs are crucial. For some couples mediation services can be of great help in discussing difficulties regarding practicalities.

Conclusion

It is clear that the roles of fathers and the patterns of family life are changing rapidly. What may be true for one generation is not so relevant for another. Whatever the research findings, as workers with families we have to be cognisant of the fact that each family is unique and this challenges our creativity in understanding and working with them, particularly around the role of the father. Where fathers are separated from their children or bringing up children alone, or are stepfathers, there are particular issues to be addressed by those working with families.

Practice points

- Separated fathers may need help with employment and housing and also support from services acknowledging and reinforcing their importance to their children and facilitating contact.
- Fathers bringing up children alone are a small but particular group who require support and understanding of their particular needs which are not exactly the same as for mothers bringing up children alone
- Communication between partners is a crucial variable in the emotional welfare of the child. This may be facilitated by therapeutic services or mediation services.

3

MEN'S MENTAL HEALTH

This chapter looks at men's mental health and its relevance to parenting. Questions of importance here are what is the prevalence of mental health problems in men and how does this affect the capacity for parenting? The effects on children and families of having a father with a mental health difficulty and how we can work with these families will be addressed.

Issues regarding men's mental health in relation to their families are sparsely researched. There is a substantial amount of literature reviewed by Cummings and Davies (1994) on maternal depression, for example, but large gaps in research on depression in men, as these authors themselves conclude. They comment that 'while the focus is on mothers' depression, consistent with the research in this area, this is not to exclude the importance of fathers' depression. A gap that can be identified at the outset is the need for more studies of fathers' depression' (1994, p. 74).

According to the survey of psychiatric morbidity in adults in the UK (Singleton et al., 2001), all neurotic disorders apart from panic disorders are more prevalent in women but personality disorders are more frequently found in men. The use of alcohol to hazardous levels and of illicit drugs is higher for men and men are twice as likely as women to be assessed as dependent on drugs (Featherstone et al., 2007). There are reports of cultural variations in statistics, such as in the case of African-Caribbean men being overrepresented in diagnoses of psychosis.

In a paper by Swami et al (2008) regarding masculinities and suicide, the authors, referring to Courtenay (1998), report that men are less likely to consult for most conditions, and for mental health and emotional problems (Canetto and Sakinofsky, 1998). Men are more likely to kill themselves and women more likely to harm themselves non-fatally. The suicide rate is three times higher for men than for women (Office for National Statistics, 2009). In China, however, the suicide rate is not higher in men (Cheng and Lee, 2000, quoted by Featherstone) but this is the exception.

In childhood boys are more likely to have conduct disorders and ADHD (Green et al., 2005). Anxiety and depression do not seem to be gender-specific.

Depression

Depression in men, little acknowledged until recently, has become more commonly recognised and diagnosed, particularly in the literature on postnatal depression (Deater-Deckard, 1998). Phares (1996) reviewed the influence of depression in fathers and concluded that the children of depressed fathers appear to be at increased risk for psychopathology when compared with children of non-depressed fathers. However, as Phares notes, the conclusions reached from existing research are hampered by small sample sizes and there is a need for larger-scale studies specifically designed to investigate men's parenting.

Anthony Clare (1999) suggested that as women now had more prominent roles in many areas of life, men's roles were less clearly defined. This he saw as having direct relevance to the rising rates of depression recorded in men.

Depression is twice as prevalent among women as among men. However, there remain substantial numbers of men who appear to be experiencing a major depressive disorder (Phares, 1996). According to the Epidemiological Catchment Area study (Robins et al., 1984) 3.5 per cent of men and 7.9 per cent of women could be diagnosed as having a major depressive disorder in their lives. Ramchandani and Psychogiou (2009) report 3–6 per cent of men as being affected by depression, with twice this figure for women. Robins and Regier (1991) and data from the National Comorbidity Survey (Blazer et al., 1994) both report twice as many women as men being depressed in the US. A study from the University of Edinburgh (Shajahan and Cavanagh, 1998), however, suggests that male rates of depression are increasing. The authors reviewed discharge data on first admissions to Scottish hospitals for depression for patients aged between 15 and 65 years old. The rate of admission for depression among women fell from 6.1 per 10,000 in 1980 to 5.3 per 10,000 in 1995; the figures for men during the same period rose from 3.1 per 10,000 to 3.5 per 10,000. There was, therefore, an increase in the rates of admission for depression for men and a decrease for women. The authors suggest several reasons for these findings. These include the changes in gender roles over the same period, a decrease in the number of men in full-time work, and the increase in work opportunities for women. These factors may have resulted in loss of status for men as the financial provider for the family, loss of social status, and social isolation. It is also suggested that changes in referral patterns may be responsible, with greater numbers of men being recognised as depressed and referred for treatment by GPs, and changes in health-seeking behaviour by men who may be more amenable to psychiatric help than in the past. However, Walsh (1998) states that figures from Irish hospitals over the same period give little support to the Scottish experience and do not support an increasing rate of first admissions for men. This raises the question of whether there has been a change in the prevalence of depression among men in Scotland or whether the rise is the result of other factors.

In a seminal work on women and the link between depression and life events (Brown and Harris, 1989), it is commented that research into depression has largely been carried out with women. This echoes the comments by Cummings and Davies (1994). Brown and Harris state that the rarity of studies of men is probably explained by the fact that depression is less commonly found among them, at least in urban settings. (1989, p. 49). The authors do however go on to say that some population-based studies of men suggest that the etiological ideas developed from the study of women are also applicable to men.

So what does this mean for our work with fathers? It is often the case that people working with fathers may not feel able to approach them regarding their depression. People often feel more comfortable about meeting mothers and helping them with depression. When a mother talks about her emotional problems and starts to cry, the situation seems easier to handle than if it were a father. Perhaps, because it is relatively unfamiliar, there is something about seeing men express their distress by crying that deters people and makes them feel at a loss as to how they can be of help. The workforce in children's services is overwhelmingly staffed by women. Would it make a difference if there were more men for men to turn to or for the female staff to refer to?

I have found, however, that attending to fathers in family sessions is extremely important, whatever one might unearth. This involves being proactive in inviting them to sessions, especially when they are living with the family. Fathers are indispensable sources of information about their children (Ferholt and Gurwitt, 1982) and will provide much information about their children if given the opportunity to talk. When I interviewed 90 fathers for research I was overwhelmingly struck by the emotion and feeling with which the fathers talked about their children, in contrast to the popular image of men that is often portrayed.

In my research I also found that the better the relationship with his own father, the more likely that a father will attend appointments with his children in Child and Family Psychology Services. This is a tricky one as it may be that the fathers who are harder to engage are the ones who need more help. In these cases, writing to them individually and even telephoning them is likely to make a difference. It is also the case that those fathers in better relationships with the children's mother are more likely to attend. This means that, particularly where partner relationships are not good, it is important not to rely on the mother to pass on information to a non-attending father but for the worker to contact him direct.

This may sound obvious but when the father does attend, it is very important to stress the value of his information and presence. To ask questions of the parents equally and not just the mother about, for example, developmental information is important. If the mother is the main respondent one can check out by asking the father, 'Is this how you remember it too?' Answers can be surprising! It is also important to ask how the father is, even to be specific about any mental health problems. It is sometimes easier to do this by normalising some of the difficulties, perhaps by saying something like, 'Many of the parents we see find that they get quite low at times' and seeing if this helps him to talk a little more. Depression may not be about current events but about past events, often losses, and it is important to be aware of this and to ask about and listen carefully to the parents' individual histories as well as the history of their immediate family. Once the depression is out in the open, it is easier to think about what help might be needed or available.

John did not attend appointments with his partner Carrie and their nine-year-old son, Bill, who was excluded from school for persistent verbal and physical aggression to teachers and other pupils. After a letter and a telephone call stressing the importance of his attendance John came to the clinic for an appointment and was very helpful in talking with Carrie and his son about the problems. It emerged that John had lost his job a year earlier and was becoming more and more depressed and isolated. He had previously taken his son out at weekends to play football but this had stopped.

It was suggested that John was feeling quite low and he accepted an appointment to be seen individually. In this appointment John talked about his own father having left when he was eight and how angry it had made him feel. His mother, to whom he was very close, had had a stroke a year earlier at around the time that he had lost his job. John was feeling that life was too difficult to manage and that he had no hope of change. However, therapeutic work focused on the importance of his role as a father and how he could look at his time of unemployment as an opportunity do more with his son. He began to feel that unemployment was not his fault and to use his time at home differently until he was able to work again. He attended school meetings for the first time. Carrie was able to work more to help with the family finances and their roles became more balanced. Bill's behaviour at school improved.

A study by Fletcher (2009) is interesting in regard to mothers' depression. The case study described shows that home visiting directed at the father made a difference and the author suggests that targeting support at fathers in these situations might be a fruitful intervention.

As noted above, women are diagnosed as having a depressive disorder significantly more frequently than men and report more depressive symptoms than men in most parts of the world. Most of the explanations from popular mythology about women's depression have little empirical support (Nolen-Hoeksema, 1987). This author suggests that the differences in the sex ratio of depression lies in gender differences in responding to feelings of depression. Men are more likely to engage in distracting behaviours (e.g. drinking) that dampen their mood when depressed; women are more likely to amplify their mood through rumination. However, a paper by Nazroo et al. (1997) posits a different view of gender variations in depression. Nazroo and colleagues studied one hundred couples from a community sample who had recently experienced at least one threatening life event that was 'depressogenic' for both of them. The researchers found that the women were likely to have a greater risk of a depressive episode following the life event than the men and the ratio of rates of depression among the men and women was similar to those in previous reports of gender differences and depression. However, the researchers hypothesised that gender differences in the rates of prevalence were due to the different social roles of men and women, and their results were consistent with a role hypothesis: the greater risk of depression in women was entirely restricted to events involving children, housing or reproductive problems. However, these effects were only found in couples where there were clear domestic role demarcations along traditional lines. The authors suggest that men in these couples were able to distance themselves from these depressogenic life events whereas women were more likely to hold themselves responsible for them. It follows, therefore, with role changes and men being more participatory in childcare, that men are more likely to be at risk of depression, as recent trends suggest.

Postnatal depression in men

Postnatal depression was always thought to be the preserve of women but, despite early mention (Earls, 1976), it has only more recently been accepted as something that can happen to men.

Earls (1976) states that the phenomenon of depression in new fathers was noted as early as 1931. Zilboorg (1931) described a hostile dependent personality as being the major underlying attribute of the disorder. Earls cites two further studies (Towne and Afterman, 1955; Hartman and Nicolay, 1966) which demonstrate feelings of hostility and dependency in expectant fathers. He concludes his review by saying that with changing social patterns of family life requiring a higher degree of male sensitivity and involvement than has been customary, men may be expected to reveal more signs of stress related to paternity than the literature reflects to date (Earls, 1976, p. 213). It is interesting that recent studies of postnatal depression in men tend to be something of a by-product of studies of women and postnatal depression. Raskin et al. (1990) looked at depressive symptoms in both male and female partners during pregnancy and new parenthood. They studied 86 couples and found the prevalence of depression to be about 20 per cent in both mothers and fathers. In a more recent study it was found that of 24 spouses of women with postnatal psychiatric illness admitted to a mother and baby unit over 12 months, half were found to be suffering from a psychiatric illness (Lovestone and Kumar, 1993). The illness in the men followed the admission of their wives to the unit, and risk factors associated with the men's illness were chronic social problems, previous psychiatric episodes and a poor relationship with their own father. Ballard et al. (1994) found a 9.0 per cent incidence of postnatal depression at six weeks postpartum in fathers when researching postnatal depression in mothers. However, the prevalence rate among fathers did not differ significantly from a control group of fathers with children aged between three and five years, but the fathers were significantly more likely to be identified as depressed if their partners were also cases.

While the above studies have identified prevalence, less attention has been paid to factors associated with male depression. Kraemer (1994) in a personal reflection talks of feeling depressed following the birth of his first child and cites the lack of emotional preparation for men as being a crucial factor. Importantly, however, he adds that this preparation in general takes place in childhood and is provided by our own parents.

What might we notice in fathers if they are depressed? Postnatally the lack of intimacy can be a problem. The couple have become parents and this adds a different dimension to their relationship. Sleep is interrupted and being a parent of a young child is tiring. The lifestyle changes and there is less choice and freedom. Instead of going for a drink after work a father might need to get home. The reason for employment changes: it is now to support a family rather than to provide money for oneself. The sense of identity changes and while some men will have positive feelings about being a parent, others they may miss the freedom and ability to please themselves.

If the father returns to his work role and the couple's roles become polarised, he may quite early on feel incompetent to look after the new baby. It requires a very proactive man and a well-functioning couple to transcend this. The change from being a couple to being parents is enormous and there is need for a great deal of patience and understanding on both sides. Most mothers will have been brought up by their mothers but for fathers, because their roles have changed so rapidly in recent years, parenting may be a very new experience and one that they have no model for. There is a real role for services here and probably a need for male health visitors to work specifically to encourage and support fathers in the early days. For many families the sheer pleasure of a new baby will overcome any difficulties but there are of course a substantial number of parents who face many difficulties: pre-existing problems with regard to housing and relationships, illness in the baby, and parental mental health problems will all make for a very vulnerable group of parents who would benefit from support. Fathers are seldom targeted but have equal and different needs that are crucial and that would really benefit from being addressed at this time.

Sam came to the Sleep Clinic with his partner Kay and their ten-month-old son who was waking several times a night. They also had a daughter aged two, who slept well. Both the parents, however, were exhausted and Kay was at her wits' end because she was also due to return to her part-time job but was fearful that she would not manage. Sam and Kay were taking it in turns to get up to their baby at night but Kay was angry with Sam for spending more time with the baby because she felt that it was encouraging him to wake more. Sam admitted that he was finding it hard not to pick him up and fuss him at night, even though he realised that by doing this he was encouraging him to wake up.

Following the birth Kay had spent more time with the baby and Sam had looked after their daughter. He had had a week off from work and then had had to go back. He felt that he had had hardly any time with his son as there was so much to do and of course their daughter required a lot of attention. Sam had begun to feel very low and could not understand how this could be when he knew he should be so happy to have his two children and one of each gender.

At weekends he spent a lot of time taking his daughter out and Kay looked after the baby. The result seemed to be that when it was Sam's turn to go to his son at night he could not bear to put him down and leave him. He felt very guilty about this because he was aware that he was reinforcing the problem and also making Kay angry but the feelings of sadness grew. Communication between the couple became very poor and he felt as though it was a question of just getting through the days and nights, going to work, and not experiencing much pleasure. Sam often felt tempted to go for a drink after work when he knew he was needed at home.

Sam then talked about his own father who had often been away with his work. Sam had been sent to a boarding school when he was ten. His father had died shortly after retiring, when Sam was in his early twenties. Sam had been away from home and returned for the funeral, but then got on with his own life. There were a lot of feelings about his father that he was only just beginning to think about, and the birth of his son had precipitated these.

Sam and Kay began to talk about these issues and their relationship in the sessions. Sam decided that his own grief regarding his father would be best addressed alone and was referred to a therapist. Kay began to spend more time with her daughter, something she had wanted to do, and Sam looked after the baby. The night wakings improved dramatically and Sam and Kay made more time to spend together.

Ramchandani et al. (2005) carried out a study as part of the Avon Longitudinal Study of Parents and Children involving children born between April 1991 and December 1992. Mothers (13, 351) and fathers (12,884) completed the Edinburgh postnatal depression scale to assess symptoms eight weeks following the birth of their baby. Fathers were then assessed again at 21 months. The children's emotional and behavioural development was also assessed at 42 months on maternal reports (interestingly not paternal) and standardised questionnaires. Findings indicate that children of fathers who rate themselves as having depression in the postnatal period are at increased risk of behavioural problems at 3.5 years. Maternal depression was controlled for in this result. The effect was also found to be stronger in boys than girls. The authors suggest that paternal influence in very early childhood has been underestimated.

More recent results from Ramchandani's study were published in 2008 (a). The figures continue to point to the increased risk of behaviour problems in children. The authors talk of a 'persisting and clinically significant level of disturbance' (p. 9), with significant implications for the affected children's future functioning. Depression in the fathers in the postnatal period is strongly predictive of increased rates of psychiatric disorders in their children at seven years of age. The disorders were particularly noted as oppositional defiant and conduct. Recommendations are made for a wider family focus in perinatal services and screening of fathers for depression. Ramchandani et al. (2008 (a)) have found that sons are particularly likely to be affected by fathers' depression, although the precise mechanisms of transmission are as yet unidentified.

Studies from other populations show similar findings. Paulson et al. (2006) in the US used data from a national study of children and their families and found that 14 per cent of mothers and 10 per cent of fathers showed depressive symptoms, thus showing that postpartum depression is a prevalent issue for fathers as well as mothers. Symptoms were found to be associated negatively with positive enrichment activities (such as reading, telling stories, singing).

Bielawska-Batorowicz and Kossakowska-Petrycka (2006) in a Polish study found that a father's depressed mood more than three months after the birth of a baby was strongly linked to his partner's levels of depression, a serious gap between prenatal expectations and postnatal experiences with regard to family and social life, and low couple-relationship satisfaction. Where financial and social support was low these were also linked, but measures of neuroticism and the age of the father were not.

Where I work in east London there is enthusiasm for encouraging men to attend antenatal classes specifically for them. There is also an interest in providing postnatal care for men. These are important projects and evaluation of these initiatives are eagerly awaited.

Health visitors can be key in working with new fathers. Staines (2002) carried out qualitative research which focused on interviewing a small group of health visitors about their experiences and ideas in relation to fathers in their work with families. From this research it was found that there was acknowledgement of minimal contact with fathers, a certain 'nervousness' about them but also humour about degrees of absence. There was also racial stereotyping of fathers and many stories of fathers and violence, which perhaps the lack of contact with fathers helped to emphasise. This was, however, interlaced with other stories defying racial and gendered stereotyping and a sense that, despite the minimal contact with professionals, fathers were more involved in parenting. An awareness among health visitors of the importance of fathers at this stage, and also that they may be depressed, is essential.

Men: attachment and depression

Strongly linked with the literature on fathers' own history of parenting and its relevance is the body of recent important work on adult attachment style and its links with infant attachment. There is now ample evidence (Fonagy et al., 1994) to demonstrate that intergenerational attachment patterns are important determinants of parenting style. For both fathers and mothers, but particularly mothers, the association between a detached adult interview pattern using the Adult Attachment Interview (AAI) (George, Kaplan and Main, 1985) and insecure child behaviour, and free autonomous interview and secure infant behaviour were strongest (Steele, Steele, and Fonagy, 1996). Holmes (1993) suggests that maternal rather than paternal security is the more potent transmitter of secure attachment across the generations. This may pertain less in the context of current social changes with fathers potentially becoming more involved in parenting.

From attachment theory (Bowlby, 1980) we know that separation and/or loss in childhood can have long-term adverse effects and, from research with adults using the AAI, the way in which parents construe their own childhood experiences can impinge on the way they manage to parent their children. At its most simplistic, a secure base in childhood transmits across the generations through responsive parenting to securely attached children. Concomitantly, losses or separations, especially during childhood, that are not handled well may link with subsequent adult depression and parenting problems and result in insecure attachment for children. Empirical findings have made it clear that the main risks do not stem from loss as such, but rather from the discordant and disrupted parenting relationships that may precede or follow the loss (Rutter, 1995; Parker et al., 1992). Painful early experiences may also make it difficult for fathers to be open to recognition of difficult experiences in their own children, and thus harder for them both to parent and to recognise problems that might require clinical intervention. Their own attachment needs will affect how they relate both as partners and as fathers.

There have been a number of studies which focus on the link between attachment and depression using the Parental Bonding Instrument (PBI) to measure care and overprotection from participants' own parents (Parker, Tupling and Brown, 1979). Both borderline personality disorder and chronic depression in adulthood, for example, have been linked with retrospective reports of low care and high overprotection on the PBI from both parents (Zweig-Frank and Paris, 1991) and from mothers (Patrick et al., 1994). Parker (1994) reviews this research and concludes that, although these aspects act as risk factors, they are unlikely to establish an 'immutable diathesis' to depression. Findings by Strahan (1995) further suggest that current relationships may act as mediating effects on the association between attachment and depression. The work by Brown and Harris (1978) shows the importance of intimate confidantes on women's ability to cope with adverse life events. Jourard (1971) comments that men's tendency to self-disclosure is less than that of women, and that women are the recipients of more disclosure than men. He goes on to talk of men being skilled at disguising their need for affection and at appearing to be coping. Lewis (1978) writes of the barriers to emotional intimacy that exist between men as a result of the pressures of conforming to traditional roles in our society and the lack of adequate role models. Even where malaise is recognised by men, there are sociocultural barriers to seeking help. While difficult early experiences are important predictors of how people might cope with subsequent events, they are not necessarily fixed since they may in some cases be mediated by more positive subsequent events, and their expression is likely to be affected by the social context of gender, social class and ethnic cultural norms.

In a study examining relationships and predictors in IVF fathers (Hjelmstedt and Collins, 2008), the authors found that IVF fathers are as strongly attached as other fathers to their infants but are rated higher on somatic anxiety and indirect aggression and are less assertive. However, they found that having less optimal attachment to their unborn infant and high levels of anxiety and irritability are related to weaker father–infant relationships.

The social class of the fathers was found by Stansfeld et al. (2008) to be strongly associated with material and emotional deprivation. Deprivation in turn was associated with lower parental warmth, which influences parental attachment style. This study involved retrospective data on recalled parental style and childhood emotional and physical deprivation and attachment examined in 7276 civil servants.

The research findings on attachment and loss and subsequent depression are extremely important for our work with fathers. These aspects are examined further in Chapter 5.

Anxiety

We are perhaps more cognisant of looking for depression in our clients than for anxiety, although the latter may be more obvious at times. But anxiety in a parent can have a strong negative effect on children and this has been sparely researched. It can also be part of a more neurodevelopmental presentation such as Asperger's syndrome, and where fathers may be on the autistic spectrum this may need careful management.

Bogels and Phares (2008) reviewed the literature on fathers' roles in childhood anxiety and anxiety disorders. They looked at studies where the child has been diagnosed with an anxiety disorder (bottom-up studies), studies where the parents are diagnosed with anxiety disorders (top-down studies), cross-sectional correlational studies, and longitudinal studies.

The authors conclude that fathers of anxious children are more 'physically controlling, give less guidance, and are more rigid, and parents of anxious children have more marital problems' (p. 546). With regard to the children of anxious fathers, there is little conclusive data but some evidence that in threatening situations children may look to their fathers (Kilic et al., 2003). In addition, where there is an anxious father there is evidence that relationships are shaped differently with children and that the child may perceive the relationship as more conflictual and less warm.

Correlational and cross-sectional studies (Bogels and Phares, 2008) show that child anxiety is related to 'paternal control, lack of affection, anxious rearing, and paternal anxiety' (p. 548). One would suspect that genetics play a strong part here. This would be linked with potential research on Asperger fathers who are likely to display high levels of anxiety under stress, which is sometimes expressed as aggression.

Marek's son, aged 12, was referred for difficulties with relationships and a history of poor attendance at school. This had increased since secondary school and he found the large setting of an inner-city school difficult to manage. He was, however, extremely able, particularly in maths and science. Marek had been trained as an engineer in his country of origin but had been unable to find work in the UK.

Marek's son was assessed for an autistic spectrum condition and was diagnosed as having Asperger's syndrome. When this was explained to the family, Marek himself told of his battle with lifelong anxiety and depression and his difficulties with relationships. His wife had enjoyed his high-status employment before they moved to the UK. Now she herself felt isolated and depressed. It was revealed that Marek had difficulty in controlling his temper, especially with a younger son who was sociable and tended to challenge the somewhat harsh boundaries set by his father.

It was suggested that Marek attend a group for managing his anger but also thought about whether he too was on the autistic spectrum. This insight helped Marek to reflect on his behaviour. His wife was relieved to have an explanation for some of the difficult family dynamics and to be able to understand them differently. Marek learned that when he was feeling stressed he needed to remove himself from the triggering situation where previously he would have shouted and sometimes hit his younger son.

Marek's Asperger son, after a long fight, was placed in a special school that was smaller and suited his academic needs. Marek himself was eventually diagnosed as also having Asperger's syndrome and, through the National Autistic Society, was supported in finding a part-time job in data analysis.

Longitudinal studies support the idea of fathers having a role to play in childhood anxiety, especially in adolescence. Overall Bogels and Phares (2008) state that if fathers are not 'limiting, involved, and do not encourage the autonomy of the child, the child is at risk for anxiety symptoms' (p. 549).

Men and help-seeking

Men are less likely to consult for most conditions and for mental health and emotional problems (Courtenay, 1998; Canetto and Sakinofsky, 1998). This is why, when men attend settings, particularly clinical settings, with their children, we should appreciate that it may be harder than for women. This is something that could be made explicit and acknowledged in family sessions as a way of engaging fathers. White (2009) points out that 'the greatest challenge to the evolution of more targeted therapy (for men) may be society's continuing lack of appreciation of the need'.

Kraemer (2000) talks of the vulnerability of the male from conception onwards ('the fragile male'). He cites the need for doctors to be aware that 'male patients may withhold their health concerns for fear of appearing needy or may ignore them altogether' (p. 1610). An important paper by Margaret O' Brien (1994) talks of the 'complex gendered patterning in the way humans recognise and communicate personal and family malaise' (p. 19). Many women are able to seek help quite early on when experiencing depression but men tend to wait until individual or family stress has escalated to higher levels before taking action. Jourard (1971) comments that men's tendency to self-disclosure is less than that of women and also that women are the recipients of more disclosure than are men. He talks of men being skilled at disguising their need for affection and at appearing to be coping. There are numerous examples of this in literature about the stereotypes of male and female expression of distress. Lewis (1978) writes of the barriers to emotional intimacy that exist between men as a result of the pressures of conforming to traditional male roles in our society and the lack of adequate role models. Briscoe (1982) studied men and women who had identical affect states, but different interpretations of their feelings according to gender. For example, Briscoe describes how a woman who perceives feeling not particularly excited or interested about something sees this as being indicative of things not going well, whereas men are more likely to accept this as a normal state of affairs. However, it is not always the case that men are reluctant to seek help (Featherstone et al., 2007, p. 136). Greenland et al. (2007, cited by Featherstone) found that men who had more of the traditional feminine characteristics were more likely to disclose distress than those who had fewer. An article by Rosaleen O'Brien et al. (2005) regarding men seeking medical healthcare looked at men's constructions of masculinity in relation to experiences of consultation. Information was based on 55 men in the age range 15–72 years, seen in 14 focus groups in Scotland. The authors state that they sought diversity among the participants regarding social class, occupational status and current health status. Younger men were found to be reluctant to seek help. Help-seeking was found to be more common when seen as a way of preserving acts of masculinity, for example maintaining sexual performance: 'Help seeking was more quickly embraced when it was perceived as a means to *preserve* or *restore* another, more valued, enactment of masculinity (e.g. working as a fire-fighter, or maintaining sexual performance or function)' (p. 503).

Carl, aged 23, was depressed and socially isolated: 'I stopped socialising years ago, I grew not to like people – see them as two-faced.' He did however spend a period of time in prison and said that there he found an older inmate to whom he could talk. He also gained some qualifications in prison and experienced his time there as very positive but felt depressed on release. He had had a difficult upbringing with a disciplinarian stepfather, and his own father had never lived with him. His mother and stepfather had divorced when he was a teenager. He was himself the stepfather of a teenager who had been brought to a Child and Family Service. When offered some therapy, he was very ambivalent and seemed hard to help.

However, recent work is challenging the commonly held view that men might be reluctant to seek healthcare. Smith et al. (2008) carried out a qualitative study in Australia with 36 men. Their results show that the qualities that men value when communicating with GPs include the adoption of a 'frank approach, demonstrable competence, thoughtful use of humour, and empathy and prompt resolution of health issues' (p. 618). The authors challenge the previous writings in this area whereby the social construction of masculinity has been cited to explain the reluctance of men to seek healthcare, or to delay in seeking healthcare. The authors found that 90 per cent of men over the age of 40 had visited their GP in the previous 12 months. They assert that 'assertions of male stoicism are overly simplistic and can trivialise help-seeking concerns among men' (p. 619).

It is possible, however, that men have changed and that as time goes on and boys are brought up with a greater acknowledgement of their emotional life, this will affect the way that men use healthcare. The high rate of consultations quoted above may reflect this. But many men still seem to see the idea of seeking help for emotional/ psychological problems as a sign of weakness and not 'masculine'.

Mahalik et al. (2003) talk about masculinity 'scripts' and how masculinity is associated with negative attitudes towards seeking psychological help. For example, men are socialised not to rely on others and not to admit to or recognise that they need help. Talking therapies may be alien and revealing intimate information difficult. Feeling depressed could be normalised and psycho-education classes could be held in work settings. They make recommendations for training and practice, such as workers being trained in masculine socialisation and how this may constrain men's lives and their expression of difficulties. Addis and Mahalik (2003) also state that men tend to underutilise mental health services, regardless of age, ethnicity or status.

Is there a gender implication here for how men behave in terms of attachment and seeking healthcare? The differences between male and female attachment styles have been reviewed by Feeney and Noller (1996). Studies of infant attachment reveal no gender differences in the prevalence of the three major attachment styles of secure, avoidant and anxious-ambivalent attachment, and this is corroborated by many of the earlier studies on adults (Feeney and Noller, 1996). Yet this seems somewhat counterintuitive in that it might be predicted that men would endorse a more avoidant attachment style and that women would be more likely to show an anxious-ambivalent profile. The original measures of attachment style (Hazan and Shaver, 1987) appear to be unrelated to gender. By contrast, however, subsequent measures (Bartholomew and Horovitz, 1991) suggest that males are more dismissing of attachment and that females show greater comfort with closeness and a greater preoccupation with relationships. Bartholomew subdivides avoidant attachment into 'fearful' and 'dismissing' categories, with males being much more likely to endorse a 'dismissing' style and less likely than females to endorse the 'fearful' style. Kotler et al. (1994) found that avoidant attachment was in itself a risk factor for health: those with this attachment style tend to suppress emotions and avoid support-seeking rather than modify the sources of stress, and this may lead to compromises in health. There seem to be no research findings reported regarding the implications of this for men and their patterns of seeking healthcare and this would be an important area for future research. It would be of particular interest here to explore the relevance of this in the context of fathers and their involvement with their children's healthcare.

Even where men may recognise a need for help with depression, the social images of masculinity in Western society may preclude their ability to express this need, at least publicly. B. M. Erickson (1993, p. 00) explains how men have been 'socialised away from feeling and toward productivity' and how the 'amorphousness of emotions can make feeling all the more frightening for them', especially when many men expect to be in control. In our society men are expected both to be nurturing and caring parents and also to go to war and face being killed. This is surely a dilemma? In Moloney's emotionally moving paper (2002), he talks of the way in which men are socialised into playing roles of responsibility but that these may involve physical risk: 'These risks extend to the expectation that men will go to war, and fight or be killed in the service of their country' (p. 71). Unfortunately, in some areas where unemployment is high, for men the prospect of a service job may seem the only way out.

Williams and Miller (2006) write about gender inequality in mental health. They quote from McCreary 2004, 'Weakness is not considered to be masculine', and write of gay men being a particular group who, when experiencing mental distress, do not always feel comfortable accessing primary healthcare services because they experience homophobia. Miller and Bell (1996) make several suggestions for improving mental health services for men, including the sensitisation of clinical assessment and practice to issues of harm, abuse and violence; the provision of male workers to work with men; self-help groups for men, and the encouragement of trusting and confiding relationships; anti-violence interventions; the facilitation of access to psychological therapies for men; and targeted resources for men in the workplace.

Some older studies suggest that men might prefer more structured therapies (Blackie and Clark, 1987; Brannen and Collard, 1982). Featherstone et al (2007), however, point out that, with regard to health interventions, there is in fact little evidence about what works with men because this is a relatively new area of work and there are few research findings.

Mick, aged 6, was referred because he had signs of obsessive compulsive disorder. He was washing his hands frequently, counting steps as he walked, and checking that the taps had been turned off before he left the house. There was a history of obsessive behaviour in the family. However, it emerged that Mick's parents had been thinking of separating for several months. Mick's father seemed depressed and was being urged by his wife to seek help. He decided to go to a therapist who offered cognitive behavioural techniques as he felt safer with this than a more open-ended talking therapy.

Paternal mental health and the effects on children

It is sad that although many of the men presenting to Adult Mental Health teams are fathers, seldom are the families worked with in this setting. A more systemic approach, looking at the effects of mental illness on the family and how the family might also be contributing to the father's presentation, is needed.

In Adult Mental Health Services a systemic view of clients and their problems is often lacking, the emphasis being more on working with individuals. Workers tend to believe that they are incapable of working with families unless they are specifically qualified. The drive to increase the number of cognitive behaviour therapists in the UK tends to support the individualistic view but, while this is often necessary, there is also a need for systemic perspectives when working with adults. They are, after all, linked to partners, families, workplaces, and so on. In fact, most clinicians have a variety of generic skills which they can employ and, with good supervision, can develop these and learn when to refer on to specialists. It is certainly essential to think about men who present with mental health problems as being part of various family systems, be it as sons, fathers, partners or siblings. Mental health problems do not develop in isolation and often are not treatable as such.

Apfel and Handel (1993) talk about the enormous importance of parenting to a population of men with mental illness and how often it is unrecognised. Workers should be aware of the therapeutic value of children in helping their parents to recover or to be rehabilitated.

A paper by Lewinsohn et al. (2005) begins by pointing out the few studies that exist on the links between fathers' psychopathology and that of their offspring. They set out to examine whether there are independent effects of maternal and paternal depression or other mental health problems on offspring but also look at how the effects may be different at different stages of children's lives. Previous studies have combined children in different developmental periods but the effects may be not be the same in, for example, adolescence as in young adulthood. Flouri (2005) notes that research 'still tends to consider equifinality (different stressors lead to the same outcome) and multifinality (the same or similar stressors lead to multiple outcomes) rather than specificity (the particular parenting factor that is uniquely related to a specific child outcome). Lewinsohn et al. (2005) also set out to address psychopathology in their children and the effect that this may have on parenting. In addition, they examine gender of offspring in relation to these factors. With all these variables, there is no doubt that the picture is complex. In clinical work we are often presented with families where there are multifactorial components which require skill and patience to unravel. The effects of parental factors on children are well recognised but clinicians often do not recognise that factors in children such as temperament equally affect their parents' capacity to parent.

Jason struggled with his anger. His son aged eight was often challenging and Jason started hitting him. Jason was separated from his son's mother. He was in and out of work doing painting and decorating and had his son to stay for two nights a week. He had very poor accommodation in an area well known for gangs and could not let his son play out. Jason was under the psychiatrist with a diagnosis of personality disorder. He had had a difficult childhood: his father was violent and his parents separated when he was young. He had had poor schooling and had left with no qualifications. He was prescribed antidepressants.

Jason badly wanted to do his best by his son. We looked at the trigger points that caused Jason to become angry with his son. These were often related to the fact that his son spent long hours playing computer games and became very boisterous.

Jason was devastated by a referral to Social Services for hitting his son. He attended anger management classes and found them very helpful. He was helped to try other activities with his son such as football, which took them out of his flat. He began to take one of Jason's friends for football and his self-esteem in his ability to be a parent grew. He attended a local Family Centre where he was encouraged by one of the male workers to join a group of fathers for activities at weekends.

Lewinsohn et al. (2005) looked initially at a sample of 1709 adolescents in the US and then again one year later, by which time 12 per cent had dropped out. At age 24 all adolescents with a history of depression at time two (360) or a history of non-mood disorders (284) plus a random sample of adolescents with no history of psychpathology were asked to participate. Parental psychopathology was also assessed. The final sample was 711 mother, father and offspring triads. Direct interviews, however, were done with 75.2 per cent of mothers but only 46.6 per cent of fathers. This reflects previous comments that fathers can be difficult to engage in research studies (Phares, 1996).

The results showed that paternal depression was important in its effects, particularly in adolescence, but that maternal depression was not associated at this stage. Later, however, in young adulthood, maternal depression was more significantly associated than paternal depression. Exposure to a depressed parent – that is, spending time with that parent – was only weakly associated with the outcomes in offspring. Effects persisted even when offspring psychopathology was controlled for. Effects were also not found regarding gender of offspring. The influence of maternal and paternal depression was similar for both genders. This is one of the only studies to look at the effects of depression in parents on their children in adulthood. Most studies have concentrated on the effects on children before they reach adulthood. This study is particularly relevant, therefore, to those working with adolescents and youth services.

In my own research (Walters, 1999), I looked at a sample of 80 men (40 whose children were attending a Child and Family Psychiatry Service and 40 in a comparison group). The rates of depression among fathers in the non-clinic group were similar to those recorded by Robins and Regier (1984), with 3 per cent of men scoring as clinically depressed while 19 per cent were categorised as mildly depressed (dysthymic) and the remaining 77 per cent showed no signs of depression. In the clinic group 17 per cent of fathers scored as depressed, 31 per cent as dysthymic, and 51 per cent as non-depressed. These figures have considerable implications for working with fathers in clinical settings in that depression is something that should definitely be considered when working with fathers (see Chapter 5).

Phares (1996) corroborates my data and concludes that depression in fathers is linked with the presence of more difficulties in their children. However, it remains unclear how far the depression in the fathers causes the problems in the children and how far the children's difficulties may lead to depression in the fathers. Sometimes clinicians can be too ready to blame the parents and are not always cognisant of how much more difficult some children may be to rear as a result of, for example, temperamental factors.

In my study, the mothers' and fathers' scores regarding depression are highly correlated variables, suggesting that where the father scores highly, the mother is also likely to. Merikangas et al. (1988) found that children were at an increased risk where both parents were diagnosed as suffering from depression. Indeed, there were 9.6 per cent of children in the non-clinic group where both parents reported depressive symptoms and 31 per cent in the clinic group where both parents reported depressive symptoms, and this difference was significant. Depressive symptoms in fathers were also highly correlated with reports of lack of marital satisfaction and this is likely to be relevant to the overall picture.

Again these findings are highly relevant for clinical work with families and suggest that where there are difficulties in relationships and one parent is depressed, it is worth considering that the other may be too.

In my research I also found strong evidence for an insecure adult attachment style being related to current levels of depression, with the strongest relationship being between an avoidant attachment style and depression scores. Simpson (1990) found a positive relationship between levels of depressive symptoms and both anxious-ambivalent and avoidant attachment styles. An association between insecure attachment style and depression has also been identified by other researchers (Harris and Bifulco, 1991). Bowlby (1980) has asserted that insecure attachment is related to vulnerability to depression, although other authors (Rutter, 1995; Clarke and Clarke, 1998) have argued that this is not inevitable because of the possible intervention of life events, which are especially unpredictable in the context of deprivation, combined with the innate properties of individuals which could influence events.

A further important factor in how people deal with adverse life circumstances has been shown in work on attachment to be the capacity for reflection on past events and the ability to make a coherent story about them (Fonagy et al., 1991). This is demonstrated to be important in work by Gorrell Barnes and Dowling (1997) in which children who are experiencing the divorce of their parents are helped to arrive at a coherent story of events which appears to promote coping and well-being. The ability of some fathers to reflect on their past in a coherent manner (associated with a secure attachment profile) was observed in my own research but was not rated systematically in the interviews. However, it certainly represents a potential area for future research, where reflective capacity may be related to measures of effective parenting via secure attachment and better mental health.

Sally and Hector brought their five-year-old son for help with behaviour. Sally complained that Hector was always at work and did nothing in the home, whereas she always had care of their son and had to do freelance work when she could fit it in. Hector said that they had heavy debts and that he had no alternative but to work long hours. The marriage was disintegrating and their son's behaviour was getting worse.

This couple decided to separate. This unfortunately increased the financial pressures but did give each of them space to reflect more about their situation. They began to communicate better as parents and their son's behaviour improved. Sally began a new relationship.

Although clinicians rely on research findings and nowadays we are urged to use evidence-based practice, no two presentations are the same and I am a great enthusiast for personal stories and what we can learn from literature and novels. You could call this practice-based evidence, putting creativity back into practice, and I feel that this is important and is sadly neglected by many who have the power to shape services. I suppose that idiosyncracies are often too complex to entertain, not fitting neatly into databases. There is of course a role for reliable data but some of it is used erroneously and is too simplistically interpreted.

I read a very moving account by Martin Townsend (2007) on growing up with a bipolar father. Townsend's father was sometimes admitted to mental hospital for long periods and the family suffered serious financial problems as a result of the father being unable to work and spending heavily during manic phases. However, there is also much humour and love in the story, and clearly for Townsend writing his story helped him to come to terms with and make sense of the pain and poignancy of living in a family with a parent with a serious mental illness during childhood and beyond. Many of the men I have known socially or worked with over the years have told a myriad of stories, each different and making sense of their lives in a variety of ways.

Family illness

There is some suggestion that men and women deal differently with illness in the family. Dale and Altschuler (1997), in a paper looking at families where a parent has a serious or life-threatening illness, talk of the differences in responses between the genders when faced with such difficult experiences. If the family had already been struggling with problems, mothers tend to see their illness as connected with family difficulties, whereas fathers tend to see their illness as connected with lifestyle. The authors go on to explore, using case material, the differing ways in which men and women experience these events and different modes of expression and how they can be helped in aspects of parenting. For example, fathers remaining at home can find themselves having prolonged contact with their children which they have not previously experienced. One father is described as having found new pleasures in being with his children but also having struggled with the intensity of their needs. This echoes anecdotal evidence that fathers who may be increasingly unemployed in times of recession will be spending more time at home and, in some cases, with their children.

Junaid was a six-year-old boy whose parents were separated. The mother had mental health problems and the father was said to be unable to attend appointments because he was disabled. The mother was extremely anxious about her son who was vulnerable at school and underachieving academically. A home visit to the father revealed a very different picture. Despite having multiple health problems and being very immobile, this father was very involved in his son's life. He was much less anxious than the mother and had a more realistic perspective on his son's difficulties. The son was delighted that his father was seen and the area of work that emerged as a priority was helping the mother with her anxieties and supporting her to recognise the father's contribution.

Conclusion

Many fathers will present with problems of depression and anxiety that will impair their roles in the family and even their ability to work outside the home. Where the problems are serious, the children may need protection. However, many problems are remediable with careful work, support and understanding. This does not have to be provided by statutory services but the need to seek help needs to be destigmatised. In some families, grandparents and the wider family can play a helpful role; others may seek help from their communities; others may prefer a confidential service such as that provided by qualified therapists.

Practice points

- Be aware that men express depression and anxiety differently from women, and generally delay seeking health care more than women. How can we destigmatise help-seeking for men?
- Challenge your assumptions about 'male' and 'female' health issues; for example, consider that men can suffer postnatal depression.
- Children are likely to be affected by fathers' poor mental health.
- More male counsellors and therapists are needed, particularly for work with younger men. Trainees and students should be made aware of male issues.

4

MEN AND PARENTHOOD

This chapter sets out to look at who fathers are and what they do, how fathers feel about their children, and fathers and their own parenting influences. In addition I will explore how fathering is relevant to psychopathology in children, and the importance of parental relationships and how children fare. I will also think about the role of grandparents. All these aspects are important background knowledge for our work with fathers and how we understand their roles in the families we meet. Many of the studies referred to are from research in the 1990s when there was a proliferation of work in this area and a particular interest in the rapidly changing roles of men and fathers.

Who are fathers and what do they do?

We have seen that fathers have many different roles, whether they are present or absent. They can be biological fathers, stepfathers, adoptive fathers or grandfathers, and may or may not be living with their children. Gay fathers and single fathers are additional groups, as are fathers in second marriages, donor sperm fathers, and so on. In other words, there are many variations on the theme of fathers and no one theory embraces all. So what do we find from research?

A number of studies show the importance of parenthood to men. Fatherhood has doubtless always been important across the classes, as texts such as Richard Hoggart's *Uses of Literacy* (1957) and Young and Willmott (1957) on East End family life testify with regard to traditional, white, working-class families in the UK. In these families economic factors dictated the father's role as the provider in the family in a different way from the role of the father in many families today. John and Elizabeth Newson (1963, 1968) found, in their early studies of family life in Nottingham (UK), that in families where there was a four-year-old the participation of the father was high, with a trend towards fathers of higher social class being more participative.

Brannen et al. (1997) showed that 59 per cent of British mothers were then working and that only 27 per cent of two-parent families were comprised of the traditional, male, full-time breadwinner and the mother at home. This has now changed and more recent data (Allan and Crow, 2001) shows that overall 70 per cent of married mothers are economically active, but of course this varies with the age of the children: fewer mothers are employed where they have pre-school children and the percentages increase as the children get older, although these figures may decrease as a result of eco-nomic recession. This does of course have implications for roles in families. Overall there is greater support for the idea of equality between fathers and mothers in family life than actually takes place. Although recent research (Lamb, 2004) suggests that fathers spend more time caring for their children than in the past, mothers spend more time looking after their children and carry the responsibility for the organisation of their children's lives. The longer the fathers' working hours, the less they contribute to childcare. Moreover, mothers remain responsible for household chores (apart from repairs and DIY and here the contribution from men should not be underestimated!) even where there are households in which both parents are working full time (Burghes et al., 1997). Where both parents are employed in professional/managerial jobs (7 per cent of families) they may be working extremely long hours and on average 15 hours per week longer than other dual-earner families (O'Brien, 1997).) The Office for National Statistics (2001) reports that moth-ers dedicate three-quarters of the time spent on childcare activities during the week and two-thirds at weekends. Fathers of under-fives on average spend on average 1 hr 20 mins per day on childcare activities during the week and at 2 hrs 30 mins per day at weekends. These findings have important implications for childcare and social policy, particularly in relation to households with two full-time working parents and lone- parent households where the parent is in employment. O'Brien (1997) calls for 'extremely good quality after school clubs and school-holiday provision' (p. 15).

Two unemployed single fathers talked of how they felt alienated at the school gates. One spoke English as an additional language and found it hard to talk to the other parents, who were mainly women. The other noticed how

*several fathers dropped the children off in the morning but never did both
ends of the day as he did. He found it harder to network with the mothers
and did not see the fathers enough to be able to arrange after-school liaisons
between the children and their friends.*

Research in Dagenham by O'Brien and Jones (1996) on 14-year-olds
employed the use of diary-keeping by the teenagers in order to examine the level of involvement with mothers and fathers. Although
the most influential factors were shown to be the children's own
occupational aspirations, the amount of praise and encouragement
by parents, and the material environment, it was also shown that
the best outcome for children, as measured by examination results,
was where there was a part-time working mother and full-time
working father. In homes where both parents worked full time the
results were not as good and the worst results were in the households with the traditional male breadwinner. These teenage children
reported spending more time overall with their mothers than with
their fathers, and the mother was the first parent that the children
would go to about many of their worries, including those related to
school and homework. Nonetheless, this same study reports that,
although children reported spending more time overall with their
mothers than with their fathers, boys in fact spent more time with
their fathers and slightly less time with their mothers than did the
girls. Furthermore, contact with the fathers was greatest where both
parents were working full-time, perhaps because more effort was
made to be with the children at weekends. However, Gottfried et al.
(1999) found no significant differences in the development, parenting or home environment of children studied from infancy to early
adolescence in relation to the part- or full-time employment of the
mothers. The authors suggest that patterns of work schedules rather
than actual hours may be the more salient factor.

In the study by O'Brien and Jones (1996), where the father was the
first parent to be consulted about worries, which was in the minority
of cases, this was in relation to money, difficulties with the mother,
or sport. Boys were also more likely than girls to turn to their fathers
for advice. The employment patterns of fathers appeared to have no
apparent effects on their levels of closeness and understanding, as
perceived by the teenagers.

Gottfried et al. (1999) point out how fathers in dual-earner families have a greater opportunity to be involved with their children.
The authors say that this pertains both cross-culturally in the US and
cross-nationally. Children with employed mothers are more likely

to have greater exposure to their fathers. However, Snarey (1993) points out that, despite the fact that wives being employed provides greater opportunity for father-participation in family life, the role fathers take is actually predicted by their 'boyhood experiences of being fathered' (p. 303). In other words, despite the opportunity to be an involved father, other factors determine the extent of this. This is echoed by my own research findings (Walters et al., 2001) which indicated that where fathers had experienced closeness to their own fathers they were more likely to be participatory with their own children and, for example, attend clinic appointments with them.

Nonetheless, Gottfried et al. (1999) point out that, although fathers' involvement is shown to increase with maternal employment, they are more involved in childcare than in household chores. The division of labour regarding the latter still tends to be along gender lines, with fathers predominantly involved in outdoor work and mothers in indoor work. Moreover, mothers continue to bear the main responsibility for the running of the household. It is also pointed out by Gottfried et al. that, where partners are employed, fathers' involvement is greater during the week but not at weekends.

An interesting study (Bailey, 1991) looked at fathers' involvement in the routine healthcare of young children among a population of 50 white, middle-class fathers with intact families which included young children. Bailey found positive correlations between fathers' involvement in housework and staying at home with a sick child and taking a child to the doctor or dentist.

The picture is far from simple and there are many factors involved. Harris and Morgan (1991) also examined adolescents and fathers' involvement in the US and found that the child's placement within different sibling constellations mediates the effect of time with the father for adolescents. They concluded that while daughters receive less attention from fathers than do sons, this is less so where there are more brothers. Similarly, sons are advantaged by being the only boy in terms of attention from the father. Stewart (1990) suggests that fathers become more involved in the childcare of the older child when the second child is born.

Some authors are struggling to move away from a 'deficit model' of men in families where people tend to look at what men are *not* doing rather than at what contributions they do make. Hawkins and Dollahite (1994) cite how research has found that fathers emphasise 'active play and outdoor recreation, skill development, discipline and achievement' with children more than do mothers, and that these are areas of men's competence which receive insufficient recognition. Gerson (1993) states that while many men do enjoy privileges, others have made great changes and that contemporary American men face social and economic dilemmas not previously met by earlier generations. This research involved detailed interviews with 138 men from various backgrounds in the age group 30–50. The interviews focused on the relationship between childhood experiences and expectations and the men's lives in adulthood, and the factors that influenced the decisions they made regarding family involvement. The findings were interesting in that men's childhood experiences, paternal role models, and attitudes and expectations in relation to future roles as husbands and fathers were not necessarily linked with how they actually lived as adult men in families. Their 'degree of egalitarianism' and involvement in family life were more likely to be based on personal experiences and 'moral, ethical, and personal choices' which were often influenced by 'their commitment to loved ones'. Indeed, Snarey (1993) comments that fathers who are highly involved in childrearing are likely to have strong marital commitments and that marital affinity is the strongest concurrent predictor in his work of fathers' care for their children's socio-emotional development during childhood and adolescence.

What do fathers feel about their children?

It is very familiar to hear about mothers and their feelings for their children: how they feel when separated from them when, for instance, the mother first returns to work or the child goes to nursery or school for the first time. But there is little acknowledged about fathers in these situations. Fathers can experience low moods as a result of these life changes but this may go unrecognised because they do not feel that they can talk about it and no one thinks to ask them.

A survey of 300 employed, white, middle-class men (Barnett et al., 1992) concluded that their measures of self-esteem and psychological mental health are based equally on their family roles and job roles. Although the quality of the job role played a greater part in men's lives than in women's, where the quality of the marital or parental role was good, the quality of the job role had less impact on men's psychological distress, which suggests that family life is of considerable importance to men.

This last point is often underrecognised by services working with men, and men's behaviour slips into fulfilling the stereotype of the 'deadbeat dad'. In the course of interviewing many fathers for research and working weekly for years with fathers in a clinical setting in groups, with their families, and individually, I have repeatedly been struck by men's love for their children and their desire to participate in family life. Lack of support and a certain amount of stereotyping stand in the way. Gender roles are changing rapidly but they lack clarity. Many of the workers in children's settings are women. These factors militate against the facilitation of father's roles.

For example, Deater-Deckard et al. (1994) examined whether fathers have similar anxieties to mothers on separating from their children to go to work. They studied an upper-middle-income sample of parents, which included 589 married couples from a larger study of families. Fathers were found to have levels of separation anxiety which were similar to those of mothers. However, fathers reported slightly higher 'concern for the child' and mothers higher 'employment concerns', as measured by the Maternal Separation Anxiety Scale (Hock et al., 1989). The authors point out the limitations of their study in that this was a sample of families who were paying for full-time, centre-based childcare and was not a representative sample of families. However, the results of the study do seem to indicate, contrary to popular mythology, that some fathers are anxious about separating from their young children, indicating a nurturing capacity hitherto little acknowledged. The authors conclude that many fathers are more involved in parenting than were past generations and are having to balance the demands of work and family. As a result, they are sharing anxieties that have traditionally been regarded as those of mothers. Echoing Deater-Deckard's findings are those of Greenberger and O'Neil (1990), who studied employed parents and their concerns about the effect of maternal employment on their pre-school children. Unexpectedly, they found that fathers are more strongly influenced than mothers by concerns about their children: fathers were particularly vulnerable to role strain, depression and ill health where they viewed their children's behaviour as problematic. Moreover, fathers were more likely to report low levels of organisational commitment to their place of employment if they perceived their childcare arrangements to be poor. These findings echo those of Nazroo et al. (1997), who found less depression in men where gender roles were along traditional lines.

In our fathers' group we discussed with the fathers the problems involved in bringing up children on their own: how hard it was to manage illness in the children, which often occurred suddenly or at night, and how to make decisions about what to do, whether or not to call the doctor, who to ask to look after the other children, and so on. These are all issues which are perhaps taken for granted by women who are on their own with children but seem to be more difficult for men, who may not have built up strong support networks with each other.

Further evidence of fathers' greater participation in childcare being associated with emotional effects is suggested by McBride and Rane (1997), who examined fathers' involvement in child-rearing activities, the stress they experienced as a result of their parental roles, and the variations between mothers' and fathers' perceptions of their child's temperament in a sample of pre-school children. The authors suggest from their findings that both the father's perceptions of his child's temperament and the stress he experiences in his parental role are significantly related to the involvement he has in child-rearing activities: if the child scored high on sociability, for example, the father's score was lower on stress measures. No such patterns were identified for mothers. The authors emphasise the relevance of their findings to parenting programmes. However, this pattern of findings has not been replicated in other studies; another paper by Peyton et al. (1997) indicates that in relation to children younger than those in McBride and Rane's sample, child temperament did not correlate with the role commitment of fathers.

Koestner et al. (1990) carried out a follow-up study to examine whether variations in the level of 'empathic concern' in adulthood was associated with parent behaviour in early childhood. Adult participants aged 31 years, taken from a longitudinal sample whose mothers had been interviewed when the subjects were five years old, were given a questionnaire to complete. The results indicated that empathic concern in adulthood was most strongly related to paternal involvement in childcare as reported earlier by mothers, maternal tolerance of dependent behaviour, maternal inhibition of child's aggression, and maternal role satisfaction. Although this raises interesting questions about the role of paternal involvement in childhood, the study requires duplication, with the paternal involvement measured through observation or from the fathers' own reports.

It seems, therefore, that parenting is and has been of more psychological importance to men than some popular conceptions allow, particularly among the employed middle classes with whom many of the studies have been conducted. However, this is sometimes difficult to disentangle from data suggesting that men's participation in childcare lags well behind that of women. Shulman and Seiffge-Krenke (1997) point out the paradox that, on the one hand, fathers are described as less involved but that, on the other hand, their role in child development is emphasised. They conclude from their review of fatherhood in adolescence that fathers are less engaged with their children than are mothers but that their distinctive contribution to the development of children should not be underestimated. They emphasise that fathers support children's and adolescents' independence and 'serve as models for interaction with extra-familial objects' (p. 218). A recognition of the importance of the fathering role as a distinct role may be needed in order for fathers to be more effective and participant.

When working with fathers, therefore, it is worth thinking about addressing emotional issues such as 'How did you feel leaving him at nursery for the first time?' or 'What was it like for you on his/her first day at primary/secondary school?' It is common for mothers to leave the school gates with tears in their eyes but can fathers do this acceptably? Many men will feel that they have to hide these feelings, publicly anyway, despite the fact that they are a normal reaction.

Men's own parenting

It is instinctive to think of how men were parented themselves as being relevant to how they parent. As parents we may set out to be 'better' than our parents and want never to repeat the occasions when we feel that we were treated badly. Parenting may be a repeat of the good or bad aspects of the parenting that the fathers received, or it may be an attempt to reverse what happened to them. These aspects are not, of course, fixed or predictable, and temperaments and circumstances play their part. However, it is important to examine what the literature says about men's own parenting.

How important is the influence of father's own experience of being parented on their current role? The literature on men's own history of parenting concentrates in the main on their fathering. However, their mothering is also a salient factor in the development of nurturing behaviour in fathers (Snarey, 1993). In Snarey's population the educational level of the father's own mother, and whether the father's spouse or partner worked outside the home, were both important factors in paternal involvement with the family. The importance of mothering during childhood for men's own involvement in parenting is echoed by Pruett (1993) and Phillips (1993) who both note that nurturing men have, in their opinion, more often had an absent father. In these cases it is the involvement of the mother during childhood that is available for modelling of parenting.

We know from a large body of research that parents with a history of neglect or deprivation are more likely to encounter problems in family life (Rutter and Madge, 1976). Hall et al. (1979) found that a woman's early experiences are related to her own mothering behaviour. Despite intergenerational risk, however, history does not have to be destiny, and the negative effects of the past may be mediated by many factors such as a supportive spouse, financial security or a high IQ (Clarke and Clarke, 1998). Work on this topic is too extensive to review here but the role of risk and protective factors in longitudinal studies is extensively reviewed by Robins and Rutter (1990). A further example of resilience is found in work by Bifulco and Moran (1998), which demonstrates that some women, despite adverse early experiences, do not necessarily succumb to depression. This is the result of factors which provide a buffer against depression, such as having a supportive parent or other figure to relate to, or being involved in a particular activity or schoolwork. Nonetheless, it is clear that early adverse experiences will in some cases be related to depression and will affect parenting behaviour.

Work by Cowan and Cowan (2000) is important here. They state that couple relationships can act as a buffer, interrupting the potential transmission of negative early experiences into later intimate and parenting relationships. Interestingly, they speculate that the reparation process works better for women who come from low-warmth, high-conflict families and who partner with men from high-warmth, low- conflict families. The authors query whether women with positive early experiences are less willing to commit themselves to more troubled men. Men's moods tend to dictate the quality of the marriage more than do women's moods and behaviour (Boles, 1984, quoted in Cowan and Cowan, 2000). However, men with negative early experiences may be less able to compensate through partnership: 'The central issue here may be that men who have had difficult childhoods are likely to be either angry or inexpressive. Wives may find either of these extremes more difficult to tolerate in a spouse than husbands do' (Cowan and Cowan, 2000, p. 148).

The issue of fathers' own fathering/parenting is not a simple one of nurturing parenting producing a nurturing parent, and the converse. The small body of research addressing these issues suggests that this is somewhat naïve in its inception. Two major hypotheses are discussed in the literature: 'compensation' and 'modelling'. The compensation hypothesis (Radin, 1982; Mendes, 1976; Eiduson and Alexander, 1978) suggests that fathers may become highly involved with their children as a direct result of having had unavailable and unsupportive fathering themselves. The modelling hypothesis suggests that high paternal involvement is a result of the imitation of available and supportive fathering (Manion, 1977; Sagi, 1982). However Sagi's Israeli project states that 'in different cultural and circumstantial contexts and at different times, both processes of compensation and modelling take place' (p. 229). The picture is complex. Daly (1993) examined how fathers of young children shaped their own fatherhood roles. In his sample the men's own fathers were not seen as good role models. They therefore incorporated into their role models fragments of parenting behaviour from a variety of sources: other fathers they observed, their mothers, and partners. In an early study Blendis (1982) carried out research with 60 middle-class fathers aged 30–50 in an attempt to span one generation. They were asked questions about their involvement with their children and their relationships with both of their parents. She concluded that the men in this study found their relationship with their fathers to be highly 'significant and meaningful, which, whether positive or negative, strongly affected their own fathering behaviour' (p. 214). It is noted by Fein (1978) in his study of men in the prenatal and postnatal period that many men wished to be emotionally closer to their children than their fathers had been to them, but felt that they lacked models for this from the culture in which they had grown up. This may have pertained more in the 1970s but is a debatable point, given that women have readily taken on roles in the world of work that were not modelled by their own mothers.

Several studies attempt to support the compensatory or 'reworking' (Snarey, 1993) hypothesis. Mendes (1976), in a study of 32 single fathers, found a subgroup of fathers whom she called 'aggressive seekers' and who acted forcefully to gain custody of their own children, often with a disregard for the wishes of the children's mother. According to Mendes, some of this stemmed from traumatic childhood experiences. Eiduson and Alexander (1978) carried out a study of so-called 'alternative' families where the parents were unmarried but the fathers were highly involved in childcare. These fathers tended to view their own childhoods as unhappy, whereas a comparison group of 'traditional' families perceived their childhood as happy. The suggestion is that the 'alternative' fathers were more involved with their children than the 'traditional' fathers because they were trying to compensate for their own upbringing. However, Radin (1982) did not find support for the compensatory hypothesis when examining intact families; she found that fathers involved in child-rearing did not necessarily have unloving and unavailable fathers. She concluded that there was no direct relationship between the behaviour of uninvolved fathers and the way that their sons acted when they became fathers themselves. A criticism of the compensatory hypothesis is that it concentrates on breaking the cycle of poor parenting and does not allude to the potential for modelling positive experiences.

One father talked to me about how times have changed. With regard to his own father, he said, 'I see him as he tried to do his best from the generation he was coming from.'

Another father said, 'He wasn't totally without regard. I think it was just the way he was brought up ... no, no, that's ... he could have done an awful lot more than he did.'

A further example of this is a study by Riesch et al. (1996), who report on their sample of 391 well-educated, white, midwest-American fathers of young adolescents and their perceptions of how they were brought up. These fathers were asked to describe how their parents had parented them and themes were identified by the researchers using content analysis procedures. The authors report that the fathers who described non-involved parents, particularly their own father, generated a weak identification with their father and were less likely to report modelling this behaviour. They were keen to parent in a manner that was expressly the opposite of that of their own father. Other men indicated how they valued the warmth and nurturance that they had received and would bring their own children up in that way.

Yablonsky (1990) talks of the messages, both conscious and unconscious, that fathers transmit to sons, stating that a son is enormously affected by his father, even if he rebels against the 'philosophical message' that his father delivers to him on how to live his life. Yablonsky goes on to talk about the enormous importance that fathers have as role models for their sons and how boys look to their fathers for 'cues' about how to act out their roles in life, including that of fathering. Phillips (1993) and Pruett (1993) both note the interesting observation that nurturing men have, in their opinion, more often had an absent father. It is suggested that, for these men, nurturing behaviour is derived from identification with the mother. This may be an important area for future research.

A father whose own father was violent to him reflected, 'He provided for us, he worked but I can understand partly what he must have been going through having eight kids and having to support that size of family. When you are a kid you don't understand the kind of pressures that he must have been going through so I do understand so he did support us and we weren't starved or anything, we were always clothed and fed and so I am indebted to him for that.'

Another father was not so clear: 'I think in some ways there are things I might be able to improve on because I think I am more open-minded than my parents ... A bit more accepting but I think that is more of a generation thing, about differences between people, they weren't racists, just slightly more old fashioned viewpoint, more unaccepting ... I think that I would have a slightly more equal relationship with children, but I don't think that will necessarily be better or okay.'

Snarey (1993) carried out a four-generation, four-decade study of fathering on a sample of working-class American men which was initiated in the 1940s. He found that greater involvement with their father during childhood and adolescence fostered the career progress or educational and occupational mobility in later life of both sons and daughters. The term 'generativity' is used by Snarey to describe the importance of the paternal role. It is derived from Erikson's early work (1965) and is used to describe caring for the next generation. The fathers' own well-being was related to their paternal roles (generativity) and their marital well-being and occupational success. Three types of child-rearing participation were identified by Snarey:

1. *'social-emotional'*: for example, taking the children to visit relatives, and spending time with the children before bedtime;
2. *'intellectual–academic'*: for example, reading to the children, providing educational toys, and consulting with teachers;
3. *'physical–athletic'*: for example, taking the children to the doctor, playing physical games, and teaching them how to ride a bicycle.

Each of these types of fatherhood was independent of the others, and fathers who gave strong support in one area were not necessarily more likely to engage strongly in the other areas. The children were assessed when they were in their twenties: positive paternal engagement accounted for 11–16 per cent of the variance in daughters' and sons' educational mobility relative to their parents, and 6–13 per cent of their occupational mobility.

A qualitative study by Daly (1993) reported employing a sample of 32 fathers from intact families who were recruited from a children's recreational programme and from employees of a large corporation. All the men had a child aged six years or under. Two major patterns emerged in the analysis to provide some insight into the way that significant others during childhood play a role in shaping the man's later identity as a father. The first pattern Daly refers to as 'vertical linkages' and is concerned with generational influences, such as how men see themselves in the eyes of their own fathers and also in the eyes of their own children. The second pattern is referred to as 'horizontal linkages' and is related to perceptions of contemporaries or peers, such as wives, friends and 'others'. The vertical linkages emerged as being the more powerful influence in the way that the identity of fatherhood was shaped. Sadly, it seems that although these fathers may have wanted to change the characteristics and behaviours that were passed on to them, they often felt powerless to do so. Another theme that emerged in this work was the relatively weak influence that wives have on the way that men see themselves as fathers. One of Daly's early hypotheses was that wives would play a key role in the construction of fatherhood identity. However, the sample cannot be said to be representative of all fathers, and the findings can only serve as material with interesting potential for future research.

In my own research there was a clear relationship with attachment style and the fathers' recall of their own parenting. Upbringings recalled as being high in overprotection or severe discipline and low on care from the fathers' own fathers but not the mothers related to profiles of insecure attachment. Fathers' level of relationship satisfaction and depression was also linked with the profiles of parenting from their own fathers. Although my sample was relatively small, these findings are worth replication and certainly important to bear in mind when we are meeting fathers in our work.

The above findings serve to underline the importance of exploring with fathers their own parenting and its relevance to their feelings about being a father and their behaviour as such. It is sometimes useful to think in terms of 'compensation' or 'modelling', although, as outlined above, this can be too simplistic and the full picture is often more complex. But exploring role models (who may be males other than fathers and who may be good or bad) and looking at how beliefs and narratives about fathering are constructed is important. When working with fathers this can be a strong way of engaging them in family sessions and it can also be important for children to hear information about their fathers that they may not have known or thought about.

Fathers' involvement with their children

There are multiple pressures on parents in the twenty-first century and I do sometimes think that fathers feel terribly pressured to be involved in childcare and that agencies may be almost policing them as to how often they should read to their children, play with them, help with chores, and so on. Father involvement is, of course, very important, but in the context of coercion, it may feel difficult. In some families, for example, a providing role may be seen as good fathering. All families are different and how parents conduct their roles needs to be thought about in the context of their family, socially, culturally and historically.

Several studies support the importance of father involvement. Flouri (2008) looked at adolescents' psychological adjustment in relation to father involvement, residence and 'biology status', and found, from a study of 435 fathers of secondary-age children in the UK, that fathers' involvement was negatively associated with children's total difficulties and hyperactivity. The study looked at associations between the involvement of resident biological fathers, non-resident biological fathers and stepfathers in relation to results from a standardised questionnaire about behaviour.

Other findings were that father involvement was positively associated with prosocial behaviour in children and was unrelated to children's emotional symptoms, peer problems and conduct problems. Interestingly, there was no effect with non-residential fathers, but with stepfathers the findings were that there were more total difficulties, more conduct problems and more hyperactivity, even after involvement was adjusted for. The authors reflect that the aetiology of these findings is unclear. Nonetheless, the conclusion is that adolescents in stepfather families are at greater risk of having behaviour problems.

Bronte-Tinkew et al. (2008) looked at father involvement and cognitive development in infants. Aspects of father involvement such as paternal warmth and care-giving activities were shown to be positively associated with less cognitive delay. This was found to be greater in relation to sons and also to infants with disabilities. De Falco et al. (2008) looked specifically at children with Down's syndrome and cite evidence that dyadic interactions based on emotional involvement can lead to enhanced cognitive functioning. Previous studies looked mainly at mothers but this study, although small (19 children), looked at fathers and suggests evidence of father involvement being important, and requires replication on a larger scale.

Some studies show the importance of encouraging father involvement early on with young fathers. Fagan (2008) reports on a randomised control study using a coparenting intervention with 154 young African-American and Hispanic fathers and their adolescent partners. Regardless of residence, fathers reported higher levels of engagement with the infant when the father participated in the coparenting intervention compared with fathers who participated in a childbirth intervention. Schoppe-Sullivan et al. (2008) also examined coparenting and found that mothers may shape father involvement through their 'gatekeeping' roles.

Duursma et al. (2008) looked at how often low-income fathers report reading to their young children and also at the predictors and effects of paternal book reading. Children's cognitive outcomes were assessed. Fathers were found to be more likely to read to their children if they spoke English at home and had a high-school education and if their children had better language skills. In this study, cognitive outcome was predicted by the fathers' book reading.

Nonetheless, the National Evaluation of Sure Start programmes 2008 report finds that father involvement was *not* increased in Sure Start areas. Questions asked in this research were 'How often does the father play with the child?' and 'How often does he get the child ready for bed in the evening?' A key point from the National Sure Start Evaluation is to have a specific worker for father engagement. Potter and Carpenter (2008) details strategies found to be effective in involving men in one particular Sure Start project. Close partnership working with a local voluntary agency, using a gender-differentiated approach, and management committing to the work were key. A dedicated fathers' worker was also very important.

Parenting and psychopathology in children

Research linking parents' mental health with children's well-being has had a strong tradition of looking at mothers rather than fathers, mothers being deemed the prime caretakers of children and consequently the main parental influence on children's adjustment. With the shift in Western society to caretaking being more of a joint affair on the part of the parents, the recognition of men's mental state and its relevance to children is bound to become a more prominent issue. A review of fathers and child psychopathology states that 'paternal behaviours, personality characteristics and psychopathology are significant sources of risk for child and adolescent psychopathology' (Phares and Compas, 1992, p. 403). A review of studies of child and adolescent research between 1984 and 1991 notes that 48 per cent of studies included only mothers, whereas only 1 per cent included only fathers (Phares, 1992). Phares and Compas conclude, 'although it is encouraging that 26 per cent of studies during this time period obtained and analysed data separately for fathers and mothers, the bias towards studying mothers and therefore implicitly blaming mothers for problems in their children has continued unabated' (p. 403). Similarly, Woollett (1982) suggests that fathers should always be included in research on families, and if they are not, then this should be explicitly stated. In most cases the reviewers concluded that the degree of risk associated with paternal psychopathology is comparable to that associated with maternal psychopathology. Phares and Compas (1992) further conclude that the presence of psychopathology in fathers is a sufficient but not necessary condition for child or adolescent psychopathology. Findings demonstrate stronger links between paternal psychopathology and externalising symptoms than for paternal psychopathology and internalising symptoms, although this is likely to be because externalised symptoms are more amenable to measurement.

Studies are consistent in reporting links between parental mental health and children's behaviour, although the varying contributions made by mothers and fathers are still debated. Finken and Amato (1993) report that parental self-esteem is negatively associated with behaviour problems in children. This is one of the few studies that have looked at fathers *and* mothers but concluded that the gender of the parent or child did not have an effect on the overall results. An older study by Mash and Johnston (1983) in a study of hyperactive children found that parental self-esteem was lower than in a comparison population of normal children, although the authors acknowledge the circular nature of the effect, and call for more studies with a longitudinal design. This study also compared maternal and paternal perceptions of children's adjustment. Interestingly, fathers' perceptions of children's problems was generally that the children had less severe difficulties than was suggested by the maternal reports. This may be because the fathers spent less time with their children than did the mothers and so the difficulties did not have such a strong impact on them.

Although somewhat dated, Belsky's (1984) research still makes sense when thinking of work with fathers. He proposes a model of parenting with three subsystems: parental personality and psychological well-being, contextual support, and child characteristics. Belsky hypothesises that optimum functioning is when each subsystem operates in the 'supportive' mode and the least effective is when each subsystem operates in the 'stressful' mode (p. 92). The most important of the three subsystems for effective parental function is considered by Belsky to be parental personality and well-being, followed by contextual support, and finally child characteristics. A further study by Belsky et al. (1991) examining the interaction of marital and parent–child relationship subsystems in one hundred families with three- year-old children concluded that marital quality has a stronger impact on father–child relationships than on mother–child relationships. Fathers who showed ambivalence about their marriages behaved more negatively towards their young children. It is suggested that mothers may compensate for lack of marital satisfaction by greater involvement with the children, although this in itself may create difficulties for the children's development. These points regarding the three subsystems and marital quality are important to bear in mind when working with families.

Henry, aged 10, was referred with obesity. His parents, both teachers, were concerned about his aggression particularly towards his father. He was also underachieving at school.

Henry's father, Don, frequently lost his temper with both Henry and his younger sister. Arguments would arise over trivial matters and Don would start shouting at the children. Sometimes he used physical violence. Kalima, the mother, was scared of Don's temper and intimidated by his behaviour. She compensated by being unable to set boundaries for the children's behaviour, instead appeasing everyone and also providing enormous amounts of food which Henry was susceptible to eating. Kalima was in essence unable to say no to the children. The parents became very polarised in their dealings with the children.

The family were seen together. Don was very motivated to change as he ran the risk of being reported to Social Services, which also might mean, as he worked with children, that he could lose his job. He had as a child been hit by his father and he had conflicting ideas about the appropriateness of using this method of control. On the one hand, he knew that it was wrong and that he did not like it; on the other hand, it was almost a reflex response as a result of his own experiences. However, he was able to recognise that the situation with the family had become extremely difficult and that they were at serious risk of him leaving.

It was pointed out how polarised the parental roles had become. The parents were asked to modify their responses to the children so that Don became less aggressive and Kalima more assertive. Each required considerable help in this: Kalima felt guilty about being firmer and Don had to establish ways of releasing his tension other than venting his anger on the children. He chose to take up running and began to increase his level of fitness. Henry then joined him and the physical and emotional benefits were enormous. As Don changed and was more measured in his responses to the children, Kalima was also able to change and to find her new role as someone who set firmer boundaries easier and more effective.

Studies have examined the relationship between aspects of family relations and childhood psychopathology. Loney et al. (1997) looked at 70 clinically referred boys aged 6–12 with behaviour problems to see whether childhood inattention-overactivity and aggression are transmitted specifically from biological fathers to sons. They measured the fathers' self-reported childhood inattention-overactivity on a retrospectively valid measure with the fathers' and mothers' ratings of their sons' current attention problems. (Young adult men who had a previous diagnosis of hyperkinesis in childhood were asked to score themselves on a reliable and established symptom checklist as they recalled their behaviour between the ages of 8 and 10.) It was found that the fathers' recollections of their levels of aggression in childhood were associated with the ratings of the sons' aggressive and delinquent behaviour, whereas correlations with inattention-overactivity were not significant. However, the authors point out that the positive correlations between father's aggression and son's aggression and delinquency do not necessarily reflect the operation of genetic factors. Environmental factors, although not formally measured in this study, may also be important in that parents who are still severely inattentive as adults may promote inattentive behaviours in their children by providing chaotic environments and treating their families in inconsistent and disorganised ways. This, I believe, illustrates the point which often seems to be ignored that both genetic *and* environmental factors are important but that they are intertwined where children's upbringings are concerned. The genetically compromised father will create an environment which can then promote difficulties so that susceptible children are subjected to both aspects – a 'double whammy' perhaps.

Results from studies are mediated by other factors such as those noted in theories of resilience (Rutter, 1985; Hetherington and Stanley-Hagan, 1999) whereby some children are seen to survive adversity better than others as a result of temperamental and other factors which evoke positive responses from those around them. A good relationship with one parent can also buffer against adverse life events.

A considerable body of literature supports the idea of closeness to fathers making a unique contribution to offspring happiness, life satisfaction, and psychological health (Amato, 1994; Lamb, 2004). However, it should be stressed that there is little evidence that fathering specifically is the crucial variable but rather that the more global variable of 'parenting' comprising sensitivity and care is important. The idea of security in relationships, highlighted by attachment theorists, takes precedence over gender roles.

A good father? Jo told me about his father: 'On one level his interaction with us, yes, when he was there he made the effort. He included us in a lot of things and took us out but in terms of that indirect route, supporting my mother which is part of being a good parent because he didn't gamble, he didn't drink, he didn't smoke but he never gave her enough money to provide her with things that he got. Food on the table, clothes for us, paying the bills, he never did that and for that reason he wasn't a good father.'

Work by Cowan et al. (1996) carries this further by exploration through the integration of a family systems model within an attachment theory framework to examine specific links with young children's externalising and internalising behaviours. A total of 27 mothers and 27 fathers were interviewed regarding attachment styles in conjunction with observational measures of marital quality and parenting style. The authors found that paternal factors contribute more to predicting the variance in their children's externalising behaviours, while maternal factors contribute more to their children's internalising patterns. They comment that this result may not be so surprising, given that men are more implicated in problems of aggression and women in problems of depression. They further suggest that the tendency to repeat cycles of anger may be especially salient for fathers and be linked with the transmission of an insecure working model of attachment across the generations. This cycle may be particularly difficult for fathers and sons to break because sons identify with their fathers. Similarly, the internalising styles of maternal interactions may be transmitted to daughters. As in other studies, the important role of marital quality mediating each parent's working models of attachment and the relationship this has with their child's adaptation is suggested as a key area for future research. The authors also suggest that the ideas espoused by attachment theorists are incorporated by family therapists into their work as an intrapsychic focus when examining the effect of dyadic interaction patterns on the child's socio-emotional adaptation.Dozier et al. (1991) propose a transactional model of attachment whereby the attachment strategies of adults affect the involvement of their family members, which in turn perpetuates behaviours associated with their attachment strategies. In the same vein we have seen how a combined model of attachment and narrative therapy may work well with fathers and families.

As has been noted above, mothers have historically been more fully researched and blamed implicitly for problems in their children. A recent paper by Agras et al. (2007) on pathways to eating disorders showed the relevance of fathers' own dissatisfaction with their own body image to the development of eating disorders. This finding was only made possible because the researchers specifically examined data from both parents and it could easily have been overlooked had the focus been only on the mothers, as is often the case. Burman (1994) describes the research focus on mothers as 'myopic' and places the emphasis in a political context. She also calls for 'theoretical adjustments, reflections or reformulations' (p. 99) when researching fathers, rather than the duplication of the research methodology used with mothers. Phares (1992) discussed the practical issues of the recruitment of fathers to studies and cites Woollett (1982), who found that fathers are no more difficult to recruit than mothers. Phares and Compas (1992) point out the need for future research to address itself to the mechanisms of the transmission of parental effects. This is complex, and systems theory in family therapy addresses some of these issues. Clearly the effect is not merely linear but a more complex picture. In general there is a need for an approach which reflects the complexity of people's lives and which moves away from a linear model of cause and effect to a more circular model, such as that embraced by systems theory. This means that when working with families we need to be aware of many dimensions. Family therapists work in teams and this is helpful with complex presentations. There is often much information which needs to be retained from both the parents' histories and those of the children and so a team approach which allows members of the team to listen for different aspects of stories can be helpful.

Parental relationships

It may seem obvious that where there is a good partnership between the parents, the families are likely to function better. Research tends to support this. This is not to say, however, that parents should be blamed where things have gone wrong as there are many other factors which may be relevant, such as the child's temperament, the parents' own histories, unpredictable life events, and so on.

Snarey (1993) states that fathers who are highly involved in childrearing are likely to have strong marital commitment. Further, marital affinity is the strongest concurrent predictor of fathers' care for their children's socio-emotional development during childhood and adolescence. It has been found by other researchers that children function best where the relationship between their mother and father is satisfactory and conflict-free (Quinton and Rutter, 1984). The research findings by Lewis et al. (1982) are still germane here. They found that marital satisfaction and father participation are clearly interrelated: 'this at once has an effect on the style of family interaction and the atmosphere which both permits and informs it. A father's involvement in specific activities with his children does not happen in a vacuum and the members of his family impinge on it. Families with involved fathers, by virtue of their enhanced cohesiveness, may also espouse a more coherent and constructive 'world view' tending towards higher aspirations and lower criminality' (p. 192). The family cohesiveness seems the crucial variable here.

Reid and Crisafulli (1990) studied the relationship between marital discord and the behaviour problems of children. They examined the results of prior research by means of a meta-analysis. They found the quality of marital relationships and the acrimony of parental conflict to be highly relevant factors in young children's adjustment. The relationship was found to be strongest in relationship to boys, although the authors examined studies with externalising problems in children rather than with internalising problems, which might be more prevalent in girls. It was interesting to note that no differences were found between the clinic and the non-clinic samples. It is reported by Seiffge-Krenke and Kollmar (1998) in a study of 198 adolescents and their mothers and fathers that mothers' perceptions of their adolescents' behaviour were more negative where the mothers were experiencing marital stress; fathers' perceptions of their adolescents' behaviour, on the other hand, were relatively unaffected by the fathers' own personal adjustment. Where there were marital problems perceived by both parents, however, there was a significant negative relation to adolescent externalising behaviour.

Previous research (Dadds et al., 1987; Quinton and Rutter, 1988) has suggested that spouse support is a key variable in mothers who are coping with parental stress. Lavigueur et al. (1995) examined spouse support in the context of 44 families with a disruptive boy aged between 8 and 9 years old. A lack of correlation was found between marital satisfaction and parental support. The authors surmise that this may be the result of the idea put forward by Abidin et al. (1992), who noted that parents can function adequately in a shared parenting role, while being less satisfied with their relationship with one another. In fact, Abidin et al. found that spousal support played a relatively minor role in children's behavioural adjustment when compared with other factors examined, such as life stress, child characteristics and maternal characteristics. However, a more detailed study by Lavigueur et al. set out to explore the characteristics of fathers who gave support and mothers who received it. The authors summarise: 'Fathers' support was consistently positively correlated with mothers' positive characteristics and negatively correlated with fathers' positive characteristics, whereas fathers' unsupportive behaviours were negatively correlated with mothers' positive characteristics and positively correlated with fathers' positive characteristics' (p. 1010). The authors point out that this effect may be limited to this sample of families who had a disruptive boy and the study needs extending to other populations.

The evidence for marital cohesion being a key variable in relation to children's behaviour tends to support its importance. However, it is necessary to recognise that quality of marital relationships and the ability to parent may be distinct functions. Certainly in some cases children will be affected by their parents' relationships with each other but the picture is complex and the effects are likely to be mediated by many variables, including parental and within-child factors. Many parents who are separated still function well as parents.

From my research I met many fathers from a myriad of backgrounds and with a wealth of stories to tell. They had a wide range of views on how they had been affected by their parents' situations.

Ralph had experienced the loss of both his biological mother and his adoptive mother at a young age. Aged 35, he told of an extraordinary life. He was adopted at the age of two or three from a children's home and has no knowledge of his parentage or memories of these early years. A year after adoption, his adoptive mother died. He was then placed with various people, including a grandmother, and a family friend. When Ralph was aged about seven, his father remarried without warning and he had a very difficult time because he was treated as inferior to his stepmother's children. The relationship with his father had some strengths: 'He was an electronic electrician; I used to help him with it ... that is the only thing I remember of my youth ... He was keen to encourage me into electronics which I think put me off; it had exactly the opposite effect. But whenever I tried to approach him about what was happening with my mother (and it got worse as I got older) he'd have a word with her, she would deny it completely and he would always take her point of view. It even got to the point where I ran away from home.'

At the age of about 11 he was again sent to live with the family friend. Later he returned to his father, and the stepmother and her children were gone: 'That didn't last long and within a year they were back' and the father and stepmother had a new baby. Despite showing potential at school, Ralph left home in his teens and joined the hospitality industry. He dropped out of this and travelled abroad for a while. He had children within a current relationship and also had a child from a previous relationship whom he said he deeply regretted leaving. He was unemployed but actively seeking work and very keen to do his best by his children. Ralph's self-report questionnaires showed no evidence of depression, a secure attachment, a good rating of his marriage, and low parenting stress. It is difficult to know how Ralph seems to have repaired some of the effects of his early life, and also whether he will continue to sustain the positive changes. Although this was not measured formally, Ralph showed evidence of a capacity for reflection about his life: when talking about his father remarrying, for example, he remarked, 'Looking back on it, I think it was a marriage of convenience. He needed, he saw that I needed a mother and he couldn't cope and she was in the same position and they seemed to get on okay so they got married.' These comments were made despite the recollection of severe mistreatment received from his stepmother whom he perceived as favouring her own children over Ralph. The capacity for reflective function (Fonagy et al., 1994) is an important aspect of security of attachment; this aspect would be interesting to explore further in future research.

Another father, Bob, aged 29, had a different experience of separation, being brought up by grandparents until the age of eight and then being sent to live with the person whom he believed to be his sister but who, he was then told, was his mother. Years of physical abuse by his father followed and he had had a very difficult life. Questionnaires revealed a very poor relationship with his partner, although secure attachment and no depression. It may be that the early years with his grandparents had had some protective effects. His son, however, displayed severe conduct problems.

A further link with separation of parents early on was noted by Mike, aged 28. His parents separated when he was very young and then his father died when he was in his teens. He felt that he had had no 'authority figure' as a child. When his son was born he did not know quite how to behave with him: 'When he was born I didn't know how to act and what to do and so on and so forth but basically you have just got to do what you feel is right.'

Another father whose parents split when he was six told of feeling ' a bit insecure, a lot of my friends had dads' and went on to say how he did not believe in marriage. He was somewhat ambivalently separated from his partner but saw his son daily.

More views on how separations of parents are viewed came from two more fathers whose children were attending Child and Family Services:

One who had never had any contact with his father found the situation difficult because of the envy he felt during his childhood towards other children. However, he told of finding this feeling changing at around the age of nine as he realised that not all fathers were ideal. Another father said that he had felt embarrassed when his parents had split when he was aged 14. However, he had at that time rationalised that it was for the best. He now felt extremely strongly that he wanted to be the exact opposite of his own father.

The stories of divorced parents are wide-ranging and difficult to package neatly into clear factors which seem associated with subsequent events. There does seem, however, little doubt that the effects are often related by the fathers as negative ones but that these can in some circumstances be ameliorated by good relationships with other significant figures, such as the mother.

A father whose father had left when he was young said, 'My mum took care of us. I don't think it's affected me that much, I'm not the only one in the world.' He now lives with his mother some of the time and with his partner and children the rest of the time.

The stories reflect the enormous diversity of peoples' lives. There is a need for workers with families not to make value judgments about what a good parent might be, unless of course there are child protection issues. Fatherhood can take many forms.

These examples also emphasise the articulateness and openness that I found when interviewing fathers. This needs to be given much more recognition in work with families. Workers can often suppose that fathers would not want to be involved and would not be willing or able to talk. This has not usually been my experience.

Grandparents

There are reports in the press of the increasing role of grandparents in bringing up children as a result of parents working, families separating, and people of retirement age living longer. Inevitably this means that grandfathers will have more prominent roles than hitherto and this could provide a fertile research area.

Van Ijzendoorn (1992) reviews some of the literature on the intergenerational transmission of parenting, although he does not distinguish between maternal and paternal intergenerational effects. He concludes that learning to be a parent may be attributed to social learning models such as modelling, coaching or other cognitive processes but that these models do not help us to understand the mechanisms of transmission of parenting models. More promise is found, according to van Ijzendoorn, in the attachment theory paradigms, and also observational methods. The author calls for more longitudinal studies over two or three generations and detailed descriptions of individual cases to elucidate this area further.

Attempts are being made to look at intergenerational patterns of parenting. For example, Snarey (1993) refers to the role of grandfathers representing a second chance at parenting which may not have gone well with their own children. A review of grandparenting and its relationship to parenting by Drew et al. (1998) suggests that it would be important to see if grandparents' attachment status has an influence on the grandchildren's attachment style. They suggest that there is increased scope for three-generational models of family functioning with recent developments in attachment theory. Benoit and Parker (1994) looked at mothers and grandmothers and found that 65 per cent of grandmother–mother–infant triads had corresponding attachment classification. However, this study had an overrepresentative number of participants classified as securely attached and requires replication not only with a different group but also with fathers and grandfathers. A further study has shown that grandparents of conduct-disordered children are also more likely to show antisocial behaviour than grandparents of children who do not have conduct disorder (Webster-Stratton and Herbert, 1994).

In an early piece of research on family and kinship in East London, Willmott and Young (1957) write about the importance of grandparents. In general, grandparents are much more indulgent to their grandchildren than parents are but other factors, such as playing an advisory role to parents, are important. In this particular social group, the maternal grandmother tended to have supremacy of role. Lussier et al. (2002) state that well-adjusted children elicit closeness to grandparents.

As practitioners we need to think about the wider family and their involvement with the children we see. Grandfathers may be very influential in the narratives told, especially in relation to fathers' own fathering and how they feel about being a father.

Jack had experienced physical abuse from his own father and was estranged from him. He particularly wanted to protect his children from the experiences that he had had but became almost too anxious and protective of them, which caused rows between him and his partner Dee. Through talking about his experiences with his father on his own and realising that his family set-up was completely different from his own experiences, Jack was able to be more relaxed about his children and to learn from Dee about where appropriate boundaries for safety lay. As his confidence grew, he was able to be in touch with his father who was remorseful and wanted to see his grandchildren. Jack began to understand more about his father, how stressed he had been when they were growing up when faced with job uncertainty and four children to feed. Their relationship became more tolerant and understanding, although Jack did not feel able to leave the children with his father on their own for any time.

Research by Smith (2005) on grandparents shows that grandmothers are involved with their grandchildren more than grandfathers are. However, the generation of fathers who are now grandfathers will have had a different upbringing from the fathers and boys of today. Smith also states that grandparents on the mother's side are more involved that those on the father's side. This can be particularly difficult for parents of sons when they separate or divorce. However, another interesting finding was that although stepgrandparents tend to have less contact with grandchildren than do grandparents, stepgrandfathers have more contact with stepgrandchildren than do stepgrandmothers.

Gay fathers

Tasker (2005) summarises the literature on gay men and fatherhood. Gay men may be fathers through coparenting arrangements with lesbian mothers, often through sperm donation. Some may parent through a surrogacy agreement, some through adoption. Some fathers are parenting from a previous heterosexual relationship – children from this arrangement seldom live with their fathers after separation of the heterosexual couple. Research in this area is difficult as participants may not wish to be identified. There are no adequate samples to look at developmental outcomes. Where there are studies there are considerable methodological issues, and findings need to be interpreted with caution. Many studies on gay parents have middle-class participants who are more willing to be recruited, and little is known regarding ethnicity and sexual identity. The majority of children from gay partnerships grow up to be heterosexual.

Overall, as with lesbian parenting, children of gay fathers are a group 'just as likely to show typical adjustment on the various developmental outcomes assessed'. Other researchers have noted that relationships and family interactions are more important than family structures (Tasker, 2005).

Interestingly, I seldom meet a gay father in the clinical setting. I have worked with several lesbian mothers but few gay fathers. It may be that if gay men are bringing up children they still feel that there is a stigma attached to this and that they may be judged by professionals. This of course should not be the case.

Healthcare professionals should never assume that problems are related to gay parenting. Lengthy questioning about the family relationships may be uncomfortable for clients who feel that they have to justify their sexual orientation. 'Research findings to date indicate that some family processes, such as the effects of parenting stress, parental conflict, and parental mental illness, have similar consequences for children across different types of family form, irrespective of parental sexual orientation' (Tasker, 2005, p. 238).

How aware is the child about his/her parents' sexual orientation? Fathers whose children were aware of their father being gay reported more acceptance from their daughters than from their sons (Barrett and Tasker, 2002). Some children can encounter homophobia in the school setting and this can feel uncomfortable and may need to be addressed by the school.

Reviews of healthcare services suggest widespread discrimination towards lesbian, gay and bisexual people (Tasker, 2005). In terms of practice, practitioners must think about their own issues and if they feel uncomfortable working with these families, they should speak with colleagues or refer on. Addressing the narrative of how the child was conceived and brought up may be important in these families with developmentally appropriate explanations being given for children. Thinking about clinic leaflets and depictions of varieties of family constellations is important.

Conclusion

This chapter has examined many aspects of men and parenthood, and the links between parenting both given and received. We have seen how important men's own parenting is in shaping their parenting and how important relationships between parents are. In addition, new and varied family constellations and rapid social change are a constant challenge to the clinician working with families.

Practice points

- Parenting is important to men, and more so than popular conception may allow.
- Men's experiences with their own parents will influence the way they in turn parent.
- Research so far suggests that grandfathers tend to be less involved than grandmothers.
- Gay parents are not more likely to have children with problems.

5

ENGAGING FATHERS IN CLINICAL WORK

One of the problems when working with families where children are referred with difficulties is engaging the fathers in clinical work. A high proportion of families are now headed by lone parents and many of these are mothers. However, in many families there are still two parents and in a substantial proportion of lone-parent families fathers remain involved with their children to some extent. Nonetheless, fathers are easily excused by clinicians for non-attendance at appointments because, for example, they have work commitments or they are not the prime caretakers of their children. As a result of the historical research bias, workers have concentrated more heavily on the histories of mothers than on those of fathers in relation to their children, and mothers are usually more forthcoming. Kerr and McKee (1981) pointed out how mothers were accepted as the childcare experts in dealings with health professionals. Graham (1984) stated that it is mothers who seek out the health professionals and who, in turn, are sought out by them. Fathers attend when asked by their partner or when there is a serious developmental issue to consider (Kerr and McKee, 1981). Sadly, these findings are, to a large extent, still relevant today. Family stress might need to be exceptionally high in some cases for fathers to attend (O'Brien, 1994).

Engaging the peripheral father is a key task for those who work with families, according to Carr (1995). He sees the problem as embedded in Western society, where the father is more likely to be engaged outside the home and to live in a culture which separates him from his children. In reviewing ten empirical investigations of Milan Family Therapy, Carr (1991) referred to a study by Bennun (1989) in which the perceptions of the therapist were researched in 35 families. He concluded that the perceptions of the therapist held by the father of a family had a much stronger association with therapeutic outcome than those held by the mother, except where the mother was the identified patient. Where fathers viewed the therapist as competent and active, providing direct guidance, the outcome of therapy was more likely to be successful. If parents' views were divergent, this affected outcome: the more divergent the views, the more likely the outcome was to be negative. Carr concluded that 'engaging fathers early in the therapeutic process, through the adoption of a competent and directive style, should be a priority' (p. 249).

Guillebeaux et al. (1986) surveyed by telephone interview the experiences of 35 men who had attended at least one marital and family therapy session. The men were predominantly middle-class, white, in their thirties, highly educated and married. The study found that the main considerations men listed as influencing their decision to enter a particular type of therapy were price (this was an American study), recommendations from others, distance, the type of centre, and the reputation of the therapist. Openness to therapy was found to be related to prior experience with therapy, the threat of divorce by the partner, early childhood socialisation, and problematic marital interaction. It was found that a quarter of the men surveyed did not agree to therapy until their partner threatened separation or divorce.

When considering pathways towards getting help and factors that influence this process, an interesting paper by Dallos et al. (1997) describes a qualitative study that examined the pathways leading to difficulties in adolescents which resulted in an escalation into pathology. A small comparison group was also interviewed and it was found that the prevalence of mental health problems in this group was surprisingly high: differences in the escalation of problems into the realms of clinical pathology were attributed to what the authors describe as 'the dominant societally shared discourses of mental health and distress; the emotional resources and attachments of family members; and systemic interpersonal processes' (p. 369). These factors are likely to play an important role for fathers in determining their decision about whether to attend a clinic or not and whether the difficulties their children are having are seen by the parents as requiring professional intervention.

An important study was carried out in 1978 by Churven on engaging families in an East End of London population. He looked at 25 referred families and visited them all at home prior to clinic appointments. All but one father participated in the home interviews. Twenty families were prepared to attend as a family (positive group) and five were not (negative group). All the mothers and half the fathers in the positive group attended the clinic, as compared with only 60 per cent of the mothers and none of the fathers in the negative group. The fathers were the more reluctant to participate, contrary to the wishes of their wives. In general there was a tendency for positive parents to be of higher social class, to be referred less often with children who exhibited antisocial behaviour and to have initiated the referral. Unfortunately, it was not specified in this piece of work whether the fathers who did not attend were in this group or not. Churven commented, however, that attendance at children's medical services was seen in this community as part of the maternal nurturing role. A study by Berg and Rosenblum (1977) analysed 60 family therapists' views about fathers in treatment. The therapists reported that about 30 per cent of families turned up to the first interview without the father, and that fathers were more resistant than mothers about returning to the clinic. My own study found that attendance by fathers at a child community sleep clinic in London's East End was 31 per cent and that two-thirds of the fathers who attended were in the professional occupational group (Walters, 1993). At a nearby paediatric clinic, however, 65 per cent of fathers attended appointments. This was a small sample, but suggests that attending may be easier for fathers where a child has a defined physical condition rather than a problem in relation to mental health.

How important for fathers is the perception of the institutional features of the clinic in relation to whether they attend or not? A moving account by Herbert and Carpenter (1994) tells of fathers of 86 families with a child with Down's syndrome, many of whom felt excluded from hospital appointments which their partners attended. One father described himself as the 'secondary partner'. Several factors may contribute to fathers' negative perceptions of the institutional features of the clinic and one of these is that many professionals working in the child sphere are female. Atkins and Lansky (1986) stated that therapists might create a counterproductive atmosphere by unconsciously sharing a societal belief that expressing concerns about fatherhood or husbandhood is indicative of weakness or femininity. Indeed, some therapists have been noted by Kirschner et al. (1982) to feel discomfort when treating men. Frosh (1992) talks of masculinity intruding 'upon the therapeutic process, never advancing it' (p. 160). The male therapist 'depends on the female patient to allow him to demonstrate his mastery and expertise, while the patient, aware only of her distress and loss, needs the therapist to tell her what to do' (p. 163). Brearly (1986) describes female qualities of 'listening and receiving' in therapy, which men find difficult as therapists, and notes that male clients have a tendency to be more cut off from feelings and so unable to identify the sources of their misery. Little is known about gender and therapeutic relationships, although it is notable that male therapists are more likely to be involved in marital, family and group work than are female therapists, who are represented more in individual work. Heubeck et al. (1986) assert that a male therapist has more chance of facilitating whole-family engagement where fathers feel that they have an ally. There is also evidence that men prefer a more structured approach to therapy and find it harder to engage in more free-style, exploratory styles of therapy (Blackie and Clarke, 1987; Vetere, 1992).

Ferholt and Gurwitt (1982) talk strongly of the need for fathers to engage in therapy with the family. Fathers are indispensable sources of information about their children, adding another dimension to any picture of the family. Clinicians are enabled to look at similarities and differences in mother–child and father–child relationships, which enhances the understanding of family dynamics. Systems theory (von Bertalanfy, 1950) states that each relationship in the family affects the others, and therapists using this approach will feel strongly about including all members and their viewpoints. Heubeck (1986) states that there is no shortage of arguments for the inclusion of fathers in assessment and treatment, and cites Gurman and Kniskern (1981) who state that the fathers' presence 'clearly improves the odds of good outcomes'. Littlejohn and Bruggen (1994) talk of engaging the father as being the key to engaging the family. In a review of research findings, Heubeck sees four factors as being important in determining whether fathers attend or not: the personality of the father, the father's family role, the father's work role, and the influence of the clinic and its attitudes. Most interestingly, Heubeck suggests that a fruitful line of research would be to investigate the meaning that participation in therapy has for fathers and whether treatment leads to changes in their self-concepts and motivations.

Flynn (1998) surveyed a group of family therapists with regard to their attitudes towards the participation of mothers and fathers in family therapy. He concluded that there was little evidence of fathers being more fully integrated into family therapy, despite therapists accepting the need for the increased involvement of fathers. He concluded that improvements could be made by having a greater flexibility in the working arrangements of family therapists to accommodate out-of-hours attendance by families and the active involvement of fathers by therapists at an earlier point in therapy.

A study by Sadeh et al. (2007) on infant sleep and parental sleep-related cognitions looked at 48 infants in Tel Aviv with night-waking. There was a comparison sample of 48 infants with no sleep difficulties. Daily logs and actigraphs were kept for one week by all. Parents completed questionnaires on sleep cognitions. Parental cognitions regarding difficulties in limit-setting were associated with poorer sleep quality. Significant differences were found between fathers and mothers – fathers interpreted hypothetical examples of infants with sleep problems as excessive demandingness from the infants more than did mothers. Fathers were more likely to endorse limit-setting approaches, while mothers were more attuned to infants' distress. However, mothers rated higher on 'anger experiences', and this is interpreted by the authors as evidence that mothers of sleep-disturbed infants feel more of a sense of perceived failure and also that mothers tend to attribute a greater influence on child development to themselves than do fathers.

Sadeh et al. concluded that fathers needed to be included in developmental and sleep clinic research. They cited changing family structures, the role of fathers in child development, and differing perspectives of fathers and mothers as important indicators of this need.

Gender of therapist: can women work with men?

Erickson (1993) points out that there are in fact far more female therapists than there are male therapists, and, with the burgeoning numbers of men seeking help, it is inevitable that many of them will be seen by a female rather than male therapist. She suggests certain criteria for women to enable them to work satisfactorily with men. These include being comfortable around men, being able to model both dependent and autonomous functioning, and simply liking men.

In a paper by Blackie and Clark (1987) on men in marriage counselling, several familiar points are made: men are poorer at self-disclosure and they are less likely to initiate referral and to continue in treatment. They place a high value on the status and training of counsellors and are more likely to expect and feel comfortable with directive counselling and advice-giving, 'reflecting their orientation to public arenas characterized by the achievement of measurable goals' (Brannen and Collard, 1982, p. 201).

Marianne Walters, referred to by Mason and Mason (1990), talks of how therapists rely on women to bring about changes in relationships.

Mason suggests that therapists of both genders are often too ready to accept that the man cannot be engaged in work and seek only to work with the woman. Marianne Walters (1987) expresses concerns that women, who more often acknowledge and express feelings and engage in the therapeutic process, may ally more easily with the therapist and thus have the major responsibility for bringing about change. She further mentions that therapists are wary of driving men away from therapeutic engagement if they challenge them too strongly.

It is notable, however, in my own clinical experience that it is not unusual for men to request to see a woman therapist when offered individual work. It may be, therefore, that being a woman therapist and working with men in families is not a disadvantageous position. Bilker (1993) has reviewed the findings with regard to the role of the gender of the therapist in therapeutic work. He suggests that female therapists are more likely than male therapists to be rated as having skills related to patient satisfaction and successful outcome. However, it should be noted that experienced therapists of both genders are seen as possessing favourable qualities for the engagement of men in therapy – competence and an understanding of the patient's problem, developmental stage and gender perspective are qualities of a good therapist of either gender, as are empathy, support and acceptance (Frankenburg, 1984).

Erickson (1993) also points out how essential it is for us all to be as mindful as we can of our own family experiences and, when working with men, of our experiences of male relationships in particular. She talks of how her own family experiences with her father and brothers have both aided and detracted from her work with men and her need to be mindful of both. It should not be forgotten, Ferholt and Gurwitt (1982) comment, that therapists themselves are powerfully affected by their own experiences of parenting (both parenting and being parented) and this will inevitably affect their attitudes to fathers in a promoting or inhibiting way. Certainly in my own case I am cognisant of my experiences with my father, brothers, partner, son and male friends when working with fathers and boys. It is very important for clinicians to allow themselves reflective space for personal issues and their relevance to the way in which they work, particularly as women working with men.

Moloney (2002, p. 75) echoes these thoughts, setting out some important questions:

> If we endorse a caring and nurturing role in fathers, are we prepared to accept that male expressions of caring and nurturing

are likely to be expressed differently? Thus, when mothers and fathers disagree about parenting styles, as they not infrequently do in counseling and therapy sessions, do we tend to assume that the knowledge of mothers is likely to be superior? Can we hear when men desire to be more actively involved as parents? What responses do we have when we sense a mother's resistance to these desires? Can we distinguish between the desire of parents to actively parent their children and the desire of one or both parents to use the children to exert power over the other? Do we have differential responses to these differing dynamics or are our assumptions about motivation to parent and about parenting capacities gender driven?

Vetere (1992) supports this view, urging therapists to examine the extent to which ideas about differences between men and women are based on sexist stereotypes. She extends this by pointing out how the importance of gender-role stereotyping affects the whole system both with relationships within the family and with the therapist, and with institutions outside the family to whom individuals are connected.

An important study was carried out in the US by Duhig et al. (2002) which surveyed 219 clinicians who specialised in clinical child psychology and family therapy with regard to the engagement of fathers in their work with families. Duhig et al. found that fathers were included in 30 per cent of therapy sessions whereas mothers were included in 59 per cent. The authors set out with the premise that there were considerable benefits to be gained from the inclusion of fathers in therapy with their children. There were several highly relevant conclusions from their work. Overall mothers were included more frequently than fathers in treatment. The continuing education of clinicians in family-related topics and the reading of family-related books and journals were positively related to the inclusion of fathers in treatment with their children and adolescents. The gender of the clinician did not affect whether fathers were included or not. However, the longer a clinician had been in practice, the more likely it was that fathers were involved. This latter point was a particularly interesting finding and one that I have not seen researched elsewhere. It may be that clinicians who are less experienced are not so confident about engaging fathers in therapeutic consultations, despite theoretically knowing the importance of this. Work by Staines (2002) on the engagement of health visitors with fathers found acknowledgement of minimal contact with fathers and a 'certain nervousness' with regard to bringing fathers into the picture. There were stories of fathers and violence which may have contributed to some of the concerns regarding engagement.

Duhig et al. (2002) also found from their survey of clinicians that those who worked in private practice worked with more fathers. This may be related to working with higher socio-economic groups who perhaps have more flexible working hours and also more of a sense of their efficacy in relation to fathering and engaging with professionals. Evening and weekend appointment times were not significantly related to the engagement of fathers and this was also found in my own research (2001) with a generic clinical group of fathers. It is further reinforced by work with my colleague John Staines (Staines and Walters, 2008) where we found that holding a group for fathers in the evenings did not mean that attendance was better. For committed fathers, evenings are a crucial time for seeing their children and may not be such an attractive time to attend appointments. However, there are no answers to the problem of when is the ideal time to run groups for working parents.

Shaw and Beauchamp (2000) have written a fascinating paper on engaging men in counselling and the issues for female therapists. They outline the fact that female therapists outnumber men in the counselling field. They say that both male and female therapists express ambivalence with regard to working with men who are sometimes seen as being harder to engage. There are equivocal views on whether men prefer male or female counsellors, although more complex issues than those of mere gender are involved. When contemplating counselling it is inevitable that one might begin by thinking about whether a male or female counsellor would be better. However, on meeting someone the gender effect is likely to diminish because other factors, such as warmth, understanding and perceived competence, come into play.

Issues for female therapists are outlined by Shaw and Beauchamp (2000). There is a notion that women clients are seen to do better than men in therapy and are easier to work with. They talk of women being polarised when working with male clients, being either oppositional to their ideas and behaviour or protective of them. The stumbling blocks of sexual attraction and working with men's anger are explored and related to possible issues of countertransference. Whatever else, it raises important points also brought up by Erickson (1993) that knowing oneself as a female therapist in relation to one's views and beliefs regarding men, and the influences of one's brothers, fathers, and so on is essential. One would of course also say this about male therapists in relation to their female clients. Differences in communication style between men and women are pointed out.

Smith et al. (2008) discuss what qualities men value when communicating with their GPs in Australia. Results from qualitative interviews with 36 white men showed that qualities valued are demonstrable competence, thoughtful use of humour, empathy, a 'frank' approach and the prompt resolution of health issues. I wondered how this might differ from what women want from their GPs and what is specific to men. The authors state that female patients prefer female doctors and a patient-centred approach, but there is lack of clarity about any distinct gender issues in terms of preference and so further research is needed.

Mahalik et al. (2003) write of sterotypes of men in therapy such as the 'strong and silent' type, the 'tough guy' and the 'playboy'. They go on to talk about how therapists might respond to these scripts, helping men to become more 'flexible in the enactment of masculine scripts' (p. 127). They emphasise the need for clinicians to be knowledgeable about masculine socialisation and to be aware of stereotypes and beliefs that may interfere with providing therapeutic help.

There is considerable speculation about whether the gender of the therapist is important in family sessions but there is little hard evidence on the topic. Indeed, it would be too simplistic to expect that simple gender issues were of overriding importance, as so many other factors, such as patient characteristics and the warmth, skill and age of the therapist, are of importance. A review by Bilker (1993) who looked at the relevance of therapist gender when working with eating-disordered female adolescents concluded that there was no consistent evidence that a particular patient–therapist match was most effective, apart from in a few specific cases where, for example, a patient had had a traumatic experience with a parent. In these cases it would seem that a therapist of the same gender as that parent might be counterproductive. Bilker talks of a situation where the greater number of patients are female, and therapists are more likely to be male. However Erickson (1993) paints a different scenario in which she claims that therapists are more likely to be female and that men requiring therapy are more likely to find a woman therapist. This certainly seems to be the situation in the UK.

From my own research (1999), it was found that in a clinic group of fathers, 85 per cent of the 40 participants had no preference with regard to the gender of the therapist: *'As long as they're intelligent'*, one father replied; *'As long as they're good at their job'*, said another. The other 15 per cent stated a preference for a woman therapist, and no one specified a male therapist. From those fathers who stated a preference for a woman therapist, comments included: *'They're more maternal, they understand more about children, after all they bear them'*; *'I don't trust men. Women are more thorough'*; *'Women are more able to understand, more emotional, more creative, and less rigid.'* Interestingly, one of the fathers who expressed a preference for a woman therapist had experienced an extremely poor relationship with his own mother, but was close to his father, and had a wife with agoraphobia. He was the main caretaker of his children. Despite previous difficult experiences with women in his life, he seemed to have a possibly idealised picture of what women could offer.

Of the fathers who had 100 per cent attendance (19) at clinic appointments with their children, eight were being seen by a male psychiatrist. This could suggest that men are more easily engaged by a male therapist. However, it may well be a reflection of other factors, such as the willingness of high attenders to be interviewed by a researcher or the ability and authority of a male doctor to recruit to the research. One father referred for interview by a male psychiatrist was a complete non-attender. It appeared that his wife had been very well engaged by the psychiatrist and insisted that her partner agree to the interview even though he seemed reluctant. It would be important in future research to examine the gender factor of the therapist in the engagement of fathers, although it is likely to be one of many factors relevant to engagement.

In the clinic I saw a woman who brought her baby, aged one, who was persistently waking, leaving her exhausted. She said that her partner did not know about this appointment and the reason she gave was that he had had to go to work. My client had had a stillborn baby two years previously and she and her partner had never talked about this to each other as it was far too painful. This was certainly one of the reasons why she found it hard to encourage better sleep in her baby. Her partner had decamped to another bedroom and she talked about how they had not had a sexual relationship since the second birth. She described this birth, which she had found traumatic and during which she had sustained major internal tears, and remembered her partner looking traumatised during the labour. She said that she thought that since the birth he had felt worried about hurting her if they had sex and that she was sure that he had never spoken about the birth to anyone. We talked about how the couple needed to spend some time together and not to be constantly governed by their baby's frequent night wakings.

I wondered after this session about same-gender discussions such as these. I asked if her partner would like to come to a meeting and perhaps we could begin to talk about the birth together and ultimately address the issues of loss that surely surrounded their first baby. She felt that he would not welcome this. She said how good it had been for her to talk and that she had not talked to anyone else about many of the things that we had discussed. It made me feel that perhaps her partner needed to start with a male-to-male discussion and not one with his partner and a woman therapist. I began to think that there should be male therapists available for fathers to talk to post-birth. I think that it would have been hard for this female client to have talked about birth and sex in the same way with a male therapist, and surely the obverse would be true for men? This was perhaps not in accordance with my research findings above but might apply where intimate relations were concerned.

In relation to this, it is interesting to read in research cited above by Smith et al. (2008) (who looked at 36 Australian men and what they valued when communicating with GPs) that most of the participants said that physician gender was unimportant to them, except per-haps where sexual or reproductive issues were involved. For these they preferred a male health worker.

How do we engage men?

I have pointed out the importance of engaging fathers in therapy with their children, and it would seem difficult to dispute the neces-sity of this: 'There is no doubt that we need to engage men' (Vetere, 1992). It is a widely held clinical impression that fathers are less likely to attend sessions, although there are scant empirical data for this. I would like to turn now to look at the literature which suggests ways in which fathers can be helped to become engaged in family work. In many ways this is the crux of this book: to encourage think-ing about fathers in families and how to underline their importance and engage them in our work with families.

A number of practical measures have been taken which seem to facilitate the engagement of fathers in therapy. Those mentioned in the literature are to acknowledge the positive motives of both men and women in coming to sessions and the personal costs to them (Vetere, 1992). Vetere (2004) states that fathers 'make less use than mothers of therapeutic resources' (p. 325). For this reason it is clear that extra encouragement is needed. Littlejohn and Bruggen (1994) suggest that specific invitations may help, although it is pointed out by Heubeck et al. (1986) that too specific a focus on fathers can also have the effect of reinforcing the father's position of power in the family or of disempowering the mother. Setting appointments at suitable times is also of crucial importance but this can apply to mothers as well as fathers. Churven (1978) places value on home visits prior to clinic appointments. Byng-Hall (1991) talks of telephoning clients in the first instance.

I carried out an audit of a sleep clinic for children and their parents. I looked at a sample where fathers were not specifically invited and then a sample where inviting fathers was made specific. Where referrals were received by telephone, the callers, usually mothers, were asked specifically to bring their partner, and it was pointed out how important this was when working with sleep problems. Referrals came mainly from self-referral but also from GPs and health visitors. The audit pre-specific invitation showed that 42 per cent of resident fathers were attending first appointments. Following a period of specifically inviting fathers to attend, the rate went up to 61.5 per cent. This was a huge increase and a statistically significant result.

A paper by Hecker (1991) suggests that fathers have been 'excused' from involvement with their families because of traditional gender roles which mean that they are more involved with the world of work and less with the emotional well-being of the family. Hecker feels that this is reflected in the relatively low participation of fathers in family therapy. She goes on to suggest ways of encouraging and engaging fathers in practice. These include clarifying the expectance of fathers' involvement from the outset, normalising the lack of enthusiasm for family therapy on the part of the father, and extolling the father's capabilities as an expert with regard to his children.

Dienhart and Avis (1994), in a Canadian study, note how there is a dearth of literature dealing specifically with therapeutic interventions for working with men. They decided to carry out an exploratory study to formulate ways of working more effectively with men by identifying those interventions currently being used by a group of 36 gender-sensitive family therapists to engage and challenge men, and what interventions the group considered most effective and important. The authors acknowledge the possible limitations of their sample characteristics, which included highly educated, Caucasian therapists working mainly with middle-class clients. The therapists generated a wide variety of ideas to encourage affective expression in men but did not always agree on their appropriateness or effectiveness. The overall results supported what the authors call a 'connect and challenge' approach in which they begin by connecting with a man's pain and then challenging his learned patterns of control and power. Methods favoured were reframing, empowering, and linking family-of-origin issues with learned attitudes and behaviours rather than approaches traditionally associated with masculine models, such as confrontation.

Foote et al. (1998) from a report of a parent-training programme for parents with young children report that some fathers feel that they have little to contribute and that they doubt their value in therapy. The workers therefore engage the father by gaining his perspective of the child's problem, 'reinforcing his concern, and underscoring the importance of his involvement in treatment. We have found that once fathers feel valued by the therapist and believe that they can play a role in therapy they become active participants in the programme. In addition, we have found that families are less likely to drop out of treatment when both fathers and mothers participate' (p. 368).

A further way of engaging fathers which I have found particularly helpful is through exploration of their own history, particularly any losses, and how they might relate to the current family situation. Gunzberg (1994) has some important views in respect to this idea, although his comments embrace both male and female clients. He argues that therapy has been influenced by considerations of expertise and techniques aimed at solving problems and what he terms a 'paternalistic model' of doing things to the client. He proposes a more shared conversational style of work which respects personal autonomy and creative solutions. His philosophy is that loss is a covert agenda for many people seeking help and he looks at this in terms of unresolved grief. Through exploration of this, Gunzberg feels that therapeutic change can be effected. Although men may find it difficult to express their feelings, talking about loss can sometimes be an acceptable way of expressing emotion.

Jason and May brought their two young adopted girls for help with parenting. The girls had been adopted from another country and had suffered considerable deprivation. The parents were anxious to receive support with their parenting. In fact they were doing really well and it was hard to see what extra support they might need. What emerged, however, was that Jason had left his previous family at the age at which the two girls were now. It was as though this had paralysed him on his journey through parenthood, as if, not having had experience of the next stage, he would be unable to do it. He was an outwardly composed man and it was surprising when he suddenly broke down as he thought about the loss of his other children, now grown up, which had not been felt in this way at the time. In the session, Jason talked together with May about his feelings and she was sympathetic. He had not previously acknowledged how painful it had been to leave his first family, despite all the problems in his marriage which he had been pleased to escape. Sadly also, his own father had died when he was young. Some further sessions with Jason on his own helped him to talk more about these losses and their meaning and to relate his lack of confidence in his current parenting role to his personal story.

Bowlby's (1980) view that depression has a strong relationship with loss suggests that exploration of this may represent fruitful inroads for therapy with men as well as women. This theme is pursued in a paper I wrote referring to clinical work with men in families (Walters, 1997). Although no direct relationship was found between attendance rates and depression, I did find that fathers' depression and their concern about their children's difficulties were linked. This would, therefore, seem to be an important area for clinicians to address.

There is strong evidence (Bowlby, 1980; Holmes, 1993) of the relationship between acute loss and increased vulnerability to depression. In turn, depression in a parent may have strong links with marital difficulties and thus problems in children. Erickson (1993) addresses this issue by stating that loss is at the heart of much of what brings people into a psychotherapist's office, and it has extra impact where men are concerned because of their socialisation against expression of emotion. She quotes Keen (1991): 'Men have much to mourn before they can be reborn.' One of the losses Erickson addresses is the loss of men's own fathers. This is not necessarily an obvious loss, such as death or divorce, but may be emotional distance and grieving for a father who was never very connected with his son.

A mother attended the clinic with concerns about her son having low self-esteem. He was 12 and had some learning difficulties. The clinician was surprised when she telephoned the school, which was mainstream, to discover that he was doing well there, had friends and was popular. He had a great deal of learning support but was well integrated. In fact what emerged was that it was not really the son and his mother who were concerned about him but his father, who was separated from the mother and had instigated the referral. He complained that his son was not like other boys. The father had his son to stay on alternate weekends but never took him out.

The father was invited to come to the clinic on his own to talk about his concerns about his son. At first he was defensive but gradually a story emerged of his own father leaving his mother when he was six and his disappointment at not having a 'normal' son. He had particularly set out to be a better father than he perceived his own to have been. He felt ashamed to take his son out. Because he saw him so little and did not attend parents' evenings at the school he constantly compared him with others and felt sad and angry. He was encouraged to visit the school and talk with his son's teachers who knew the boy well and were very positive about his progress. Having this opportunity to talk with the teachers and hear a different narrative enabled him to see his son in another light and he began to engage in activities outside the home.

John Byng-Hall (1991) talks about how one of the roles of a therapist is to create an environment which is a sufficiently secure base from which family members can explore their own attachments. From attachment theory we know that only when a situation feels sufficiently safe can exploration be fully carried out. An initial session must give sufficient time in which to get in touch with 'the pain in the family'. Byng-Hall states that the distress increases attachment behaviour and opens up new possibilities of being cared for. Families, and fathers in particular, often drop out of therapy and this may be to do with not feeling sufficiently cared for or secure. The aim of the therapist is to 'provide a secure base in which it is safe enough to reconnect with old memories that are resonating with current themes'. If the attachment mechanism is dysfunctional in the parents, it is likely that the children's ability to form healthy attachments will be affected. Bringing men into the picture and holding them in therapy seems crucial. An 'avoidant' or 'dismissing' attachment style may lead to poorer engagement in therapy (Biringen, 1994). Dozier (1991) found that a clinical group of patients with a 'dismissing' style of attachment was more likely to be rejecting of treatment providers, to engage less in self-disclosure and to make less good use of treatment than other groups. Work by Dallos (2006) echoes these ideas of blending attachment and systemic theories.

Mick had separated from his girlfriend. One of his two children, a son who was four, was finding the situation very difficult and was referred by his mother who was concerned about him. He was wetting the bed and often awake at night. Mick attended some sessions with his ex-partner but was offered a session alone which he took up. He sobbed as he told of his own father leaving him when he was also four. He had no siblings and had always felt angry and upset about his father's behaviour. He also missed him as he had moved to another country. Mick's big concern was that he would become like his father and lose touch with his son, almost as if he had no control over how things would turn out. We talked about how his situation was different from his father's and how he could in fact make sure that his relationship with his son was maintained but that this would require effort. His ex-partner complained that Mick was unreliable with regard to contact and would let his children down. He also missed appointments with the therapist. Mick had to look at the gap between what he wanted and what he was actually doing as a father.

Fletcher and Visser (2008) write about the role of Family Relationship Centres in Australia. They argue that some service providers' beliefs about men's emotions – which may be somewhat stereotyped – can inhibit fathers' engagement and reduce the effectiveness of services. The authors argue that 'self-reflective capacities' should be part of professional competencies. Enabling workers to look at their own beliefs and attachments is very important and particularly so when working with fathers who may be less easy to engage and to keep engaged.

Work by Berlyn et al. (2008) in a piece on the evaluation of engaging fathers in Child and Family Services in Australia found that father participation was improved by flexible hours, male facilitators, father-specific services, marketing in male spaces, using male-friendly language and creating male-friendly service venues. They also commented that fathers were alienated by experts and a highly structured programme format and preferred more informal hands-on activities. A facilitator who was male, who was a father himself and who shared personal experiences was also favoured.

In my own research with 40 fathers at a children's hospital in London's East End, I looked at a number of factors which might influence men's attendance with their children at a Child and Family Consultation Service. These included looking at their mental health, attachment, marital satisfaction and social class. The group comprised twenty fathers of girls and twenty of boys and the children were aged between three and nine years. Twenty-seven fathers were white and the remainder were from minority cultures. Fourteen fathers were from Social Classes I–III nm and 26 from Social Classes IIIm–V. Six of the fathers were living apart from their children.

Fathers were interviewed using a semi-structured interview in conjunction with an adapted version of a parenting interview schedule. The fathers were also asked to complete standardised questionnaires on their current mental health, general health, recalled parenting by their mother and their father, parenting stress, attachment style, their child's behaviour, and their marital state.

Nearly 75 per cent of the sample said that they thought it was important for fathers to attend their child's appointments. Fathers were also asked why they thought it might be difficult for some men to attend. Many interesting reasons were given for men not attending clinic sessions. Work was frequently cited and other reasons mentioned were feeling awkward or redundant, having their masculinity attacked, feeling that the clinic atmosphere was particularly controlled by women, not wanting to admit to problems, children being closer to their mothers, and feeling it was 'not their business'. 'Men are lazy and ignorant and can't discuss their feelings' was one man's opinion. Another felt that men thought that things would sort themselves out without intervention. There were further comments about men being more secretive, feeling that the children were not their responsibility and being too macho, and about women being quick 'to take the burden'.

Often workers say that fathers do not attend appointments because of work commitments. However, mothers have work commitments too. It is also the case that many employers will now give paid time off for appointments with children, certainly in higher-status jobs. One father I met, however, who was a scaffolder, found it really difficult to attend appointments because he had money docked if he took time off. This was resolved by arranging evening appointments.

Correlations with percentage of attendance showed no statistically significant links with the age of the child, social class, the extent of the problems, the father's level of concern, parenting stress, and depression. However, there was a link between the extent to which family tasks were shared and attendance, indicating that fathers who share the parenting load are more likely to attend clinic sessions with their children. There were also statistical trends to suggest that lower rates of marital satisfaction reported by the father or mother were associated with lower rates of attendance. This possibly indicates a mediating role on the part of the mother with regard to the father's attendance.

Results showed no relationship between fathers' recalled relationships with their mothers and attendance, but their recalled memory of the quality of their relationship with their own fathers was a highly significant factor in attendance. Those who recalled their own fathers as 'good' fathers were much more likely to have higher attendance rates.

Larry was a father who did not attend clinic appointments with his ex-partner. However, he agreed to be interviewed for research. He described an exceptionally poor relationship with his own father: 'We never saw much of him, he was with other women, never spent any time with us, never bought us anything, put drink before anything else.' However, he had a strong protective factor in his life, which was his relationship with his mother: 'No one can separate me from my mother. I'd do anything for my mum.' He was regularly beaten by his father, and his parents separated when he was in primary school. Larry went into care but the man who ran the children's home 'was like a dad, taught me everything I know'.

Larry had been devastated by the loss of his children whom he saw once every two weeks. On questionnaires he scored as being depressed and also avoidantly attached. But he had friends whom he saw on a daily basis, which was positive, and it seemed that although damaged by his relationship with his father his relationships with his mother and a father figure had been positive experiences. It is possible that Larry could have benefited from some therapeutic input and by coming for the research interview he was, I felt, thinking about this. Certainly he showed the ability to reflect upon his life and how it had gone but was also wary of the painful memories that might be evoked by more sustained talking.

Interestingly, of the 10 men whose attendance was poor or who did not attend at all, 70 per cent reported insecure attachment profiles. Of the 19 men who attended 100 per cent of their child's appointments, 15 completed the self-report questionnaires on attachment and 10 were rated as securely attached. Poor attenders were significantly more likely to have experienced a separation of some kind in their childhood or teenage years. Fathers who had experienced parental divorce or separation during childhood or teenage years were less likely to attend appointments than those from non-divorced families. However, of the six non-resident fathers, only one was a complete non-attender.

Carl was in his twenties and lived some of the time with his mother and some of the time with his family. His daughter, aged four, was referred with behaviour problems. Carl's father had also left when he was very small, although Carl reflected that he did not think that this had affected him that much: 'I'm not the only one in the world.' However, he did go on to mention that things might have been better had he had a father around: 'I might have viewed things differently.' He had a very close relationship with his mother: 'Whenever I need her basically she's there.'

Carl was categorised as 'avoidant' on an attachment questionnaire and mildly depressed on a depression inventory. His relationship with his partner was rated as 'severe' on a marital questionnaire.

Carl had attended very few clinic appointments. He felt that the situation with regard to his daughter had improved but that work got in the way of attending appointments. He was, in fact, unemployed at the time of the interview but was looking for work and was trained as a plasterer. He said that he felt that a lot of men would feel 'intimidated' by the clinic and would worry about saying the wrong thing. For a short period following the interview Carl attended appointments but then became a non-attender.

In contrast, Kevin, a father in a manual job who worked full-time, attended all the appointments with his daughter, aged eight, who had been referred with anxiety symptoms. He reported a good marriage, did not report any symptoms of depression, and on a questionnaire rated high care from his father and his mother in childhood. Of his father he said, 'He was always there any time I needed him. As a teenager I was a bit rebellious but not less close to him.' Kevin presented as a caring and concerned father and was easily engaged in the therapeutic process.

These findings are from a limited sample size and require replication with larger numbers. However, a number of possible implications for those working therapeutically with families in child and family settings emerge. The results clearly point to the father's own history of relationships playing a significant role in determining their attendance. Cowan et al. (1996) emphasise the need for family therapists to look at intrapsychic factors in the parents (internal working models of intimate family relationships) when thinking about changes in dyadic interaction patterns which in turn relate to children's socio-emotional adaptation. In particular, the finding in my research that the father's history with his own father is linked with attendance rates may be of paramount importance. We have seen that fathers who recall more positive fathering from their own fathers are more likely to attend clinic appointments; those who attend less often are more likely to have experienced parental divorce themselves, and report less satisfying marriages with their own partner. The small group of fully attending fathers were more likely to be securely attached, and those who were non-attenders or poor attenders were more likely to be avoidantly attached.

It may be, therefore, that the energies of therapists should be directed to creative ways of encouraging attendance by fathers. This would inevitably be difficult in relation to those families where the fathers is a complete non-attender, but where there are fathers who are poor attenders, active engagement strategies by the therapist might be crucial. In my own research it was notable that fathers were often positively engaged by participating in the research interview and sometimes subsequently attended a family appointment where they had not previously been engaged in family work with their child. This indicates that taking a special interest in the father and his history and, in a clinic session, positively connoting his role, is likely to be very important. In the light of the finding from this research that those fathers who were poor attenders were more likely to report lower rates of marital satisfaction, it would also seem important to address this by making direct contact with the fathers themselves, rather than through the mother, and connoting the importance of their contribution to clinical work with their child. The attachment paradigm for engaging families outlined by Byng-Hall (1991) is likely to be highly relevant for fathers with poor histories of relationships with their own fathers. However, the work required to modify insecure attachments to more secure models and rewriting narratives may be substantial.

It therefore seems likely that fathers' experience of their own fathering is an important factor in attendance patterns of fathers at appointments where their child is referred with psychological difficulties. Despite common assumptions by clinicians that fathers may be too busy to attend and that attendance can be excused, clinicians should look beyond these reasons and attempt to work on making fathers feel that their role is far from peripheral. Exploration of their relationships with their own fathers can often be fruitful and help them to think about their roles in relation to their own children.

Young fathers

It is hard to know just how many young fathers there are. Although the UK has the highest rates of teenage births in Europe, the records are not complete because the mother does not always include the name of the father in the birth details. What we do know, however, is that young fathers tend to come from lower socio-economic groups and to leave school early. They will often have housing and employment needs. Unfortunately services have a tendency to focus on the mothers and struggle to find effective ways of including young fathers, who can be wary of involvement in services, despite evidence (Lamb and Lewis, 2004) refuting the view of disinterested or 'feckless' young fathers. Sherriff (2007), in a beautifully written paper on young fathers, highlights the issues of services seeming 'unmanly' for some young men. Sherriff points out issues of masculinity and says that sometimes promoting services for males 'is championed as a way of redressing the perceived excesses of feminism, rather than part of responding to a more complex understanding of how masculinities and femininities function in current society' (p. 7). He goes on to say that, from his perspective, 'it would appear that a working knowledge of such ideas and how they might impact on young men and women in relation to fatherhood would be valuable for practitioners.' (p. 7).

Young fathers are, therefore, a specific but nonetheless diverse group. They are vulnerable in that they do not have economic security, and being a father may exacerbate this. In addition, they often do not stay with the child's mother. But research shows that they are often motivated and can be very involved in childcare, especially if unemployed (Lewis, 2000, p. 8). However, unemployed fathers can often see themselves as failing to provide and do not always appear to enjoy their greater involvement in childcare. Having somewhere to live is an additional problem. Some young fathers feel that if they are separated from their child's mother, they should have a place where they can have their child to stay.

Right from the beginning in the antenatal clinics, it is important to engage fathers. Young fathers complain that they are excluded and intimidated by services. Publications are also seen as being biased towards mothers. Practical suggestions for those working in this area – such as making sure the father is offered a chair at any consultation and making eye contact with both parents when talking with a couple – are very basic but important.

Futris and Schoppe-Sullivan (2007) examined relationships among 74 US adolescent mothers' perceptions of barriers to fathers' engagement, parenting alliance strength, and non-resident fathers' engagement in caregiving and nurturing activities with their children. Findings suggest that it is important to help young parents strengthen their coparenting relationship in order to foster fathers' engagement with their children. The authors suggest that programmes promoting father engagement should try to foster relationship-maintenance skills to enhance the parenting alliance. These skills would include the enhancement of valuing and respecting the parenting role, and communication and conflict management. This may, however, be ineffective, as the period of romantic involvement may have dissolved following the birth. Preparation for employment may sometimes be more helpful to young fathers.

Working without fathers

It is often the case when working with families that fathers do not attend sessions. Of course there are several reasons why this may happen: fathers may not live with the family, they may be out of touch with the family, they may be in prison or they may be working. In some rarer cases they may have died. Sometimes their whereabouts are not known. Fathers may simply not see the need to prioritise appointments and this may be seen as the mother's role. They may be anxious about appointments with professionals and nervous about 'being judged', particularly in predominantly female settings. Alternatively, if clinicians do not make it clear that fathers' attendance is welcome and that there is an expectation of attendance, this may also affect the situation.

In some cases mothers may even block the attendance of their children's father at appointments, perhaps because they feel the need to use the time to talk for themselves, because they are angry with the father or because they deem the relationship too poor for a joint interview to be constructive. In these cases it may be wise to communicate with the father direct. Alternatively, if the situation is very fraught and the communication between the parents is poor, an appointment can be arranged to see the father alone. What is to be avoided is the situation where parental rows and differences are enacted in front of the children so, if this is a potential concern, it might also be good to see the parents together but separately from the children.

Working without fathers requires skill. It is often easier to ignore the issues but 'In his own mind no child is "without a father". In the absence of a given story he will make up his own' (Kraemer, 2005, p. 114).

Kraemer goes on to say that 'when the father is rarely or never seen, the child depends on his mother or other relatives to inform him'. This can of course create problems if the father is framed as nothing but bad, leaving any child, but particularly a male child, feeling that this is his inevitable inheritance. Kraemer stresses the importance of keeping good memories alive so that the child has some positive images of the father. It is important clinically to try and elicit some good memories when working without fathers and not simply to listen to a catalogue of wrongdoings. This may make for complexities because, if the positive aspects are emphasised, the child may wonder why the parents did not stay together. The therapeutic task is to make sense of the broken relationship and create a narrative that has meaning for the child at that stage of his or her life. Narratives can then evolve and adapt throughout life with maturity and life experiences.

Absent fathers should not be ignored. As said above, there can be many different reasons for their absence, and the approach will need to be tailored accordingly. However, even if the father is not physically in the session, he can be brought into the room. Sometimes a chair can be set out for the absent father. Questions such as 'If your dad were here, what would he be saying?' might be used. This sort of question can, where appropriate, open up new dialogues in family sessions. However, where fathers are absent for whatever reason, questions may open up stories of grief, anger, resentment, bitterness and also love. These can be challenging areas for therapists to work with and require considerable skill.

Conclusion

This chapter has attempted to address key issues for all of us who work with families, be it as social workers, psychologists, health visitors, midwives, teachers, family centre workers, and so on. I have tried to emphasise the need to keep fathers in mind whether they are present or absent, positive or negative influences, and whatever role they play in the family narrative. Some ideas are simple and practical; others are about addressing our own beliefs, and some of the work requires therapeutic skills. Whatever is needed, there are shortcomings that can be addressed to make our services more responsive to the world of fathers and their families.

Practice points

- Think about your own experience of fathers. What beliefs do you hold about fathers? Which may help engagement (e.g. fathers as well as mothers are important in a child's development) and which may be less helpful (e.g. fathers are not a source of information about child development; fathers may be violent)?
- Appointment letters emphasising the importance of both parents attending are important. If a father does not attend following an

invitation, make a point of speaking to him directly. Do not rely on the mother to convey information.

- If parents are separated, communicate with both parents if appropriate. Invite separated fathers with or without their ex-partner but make efforts to engage them where appropriate.
- In sessions emphasise the importance of the father in the family and in relation to developmental outcomes in their children and therapeutic outcomes for the family. Talk to the father about the child's history. What does he remember that may be different from what the mother remembers?
- Think about the father's life experience. Ask him about his experience of fathering and being parented. Does he have significant stresses, such as work-related problems?
- Fathers can benefit from being invited to developmental checks when their children are young. Once they are in school, there are many opportunities for getting fathers involved.
- Recruit men to work with fathers, especially in Children's Centres.

6

WORKING WITH MEN IN GROUPS

We have seen in Chapter 5 the importance of engaging fathers in therapeutic consultations with their families when the child is the referred patient. However, there are other ways of working with and involving fathers, and this chapter sets out to look at groups for fathers in different settings.

Although there are many groups set up for men, and the numbers are increasing, there is little research in this area. Groups for men range from 'get- togethers' for dads at Family Centres, which principally focus on activities with children, to groups which are run within men's prisons and which are highly structured and specific in the issues they address and require a high level of clinical skills in the workers. There is certainly a feeling that men's groups are a positive idea, but there needs to be more evidence to support this. Recent work on parenting interventions with fathers (Burgess, 2009) talks of very poor methodology in this area and certainly the literature is limited and more research is required. This is endorsed by a meta-analysis study of the effectiveness of resident fathering programmes (Holmes et al., 2010). The authors conclude that there is a dearth of work in this area and that more research is needed into fathering education programmes.

Several authors have noted the importance of involving fathers in parent- training programmes. As early as 1985 Webster-Stratton ran groups comparing father-involved families where fathers attended parent-training groups and father-absent families where only mothers attended sessions. At one year follow-up the former families showed significantly more improvement in their children's behaviour. Coplin and Houts (1991), however, discuss how the involvement of both parents enhances the effects of parent training. It may be that, in this type of group, the attendance of both parents enhances what is learned because they go away and discuss what they have done in the group. However, the experience of many workers on parenting programmes is that the majority of attendees are mothers. This can then lead to fathers feeling isolated or, as one father said, being fearful of dominating the group.

John chose to come to a fathers' group and expressed his fears about dominating a mixed group, feeling worried that the women would defer to a man and that he would end up taking over.

Moran and Ghate (2005) echo this in a research review on the effectiveness of parenting support programmes. They raise the question of whether results are better working with fathers separately or together with partners, and they underline the need for more research.

Hari who was a single father said that he was shy of women and preferred to be able to come to a men's group.

Tiano and McNeil (2005) examine research looking at father participation in behavioural parent training, both individually and in group programmes (specifically Triple P and Webster-Stratton), and point out that the existing body of research is insufficient to draw meaningful conclusions. They call for more methodologically sound research regarding the inclusion of fathers in parenting groups and the outcomes.

In a US study, Bagner and Eyberg (2003) looked at 107 families who came to parent-training groups. Results were analysed according to three groups: involved fathers, who lived with the child and attended at least some sessions (56 families), uninvolved fathers, who lived with the child and did not attend sessions (16 families), and absent fathers, who did not live with the child (35 families). The overall attendance rate of fathers was high (78 per cent). The authors suggest that 'when encouraged and given the opportunity to be involved in treatment, fathers are likely to attend treatment sessions at a rate similar to their child's mother' (p. 603). Sessions were held in the evening and at the weekend to enhance attendance. Results showed that father participation in the programme may not affect immediate outcome but at four months follow-up there are indications that beneficial effects may have been helped to be maintained. However, mothers in father-involved families reported maintenance of treatment gains, whereas mothers in absent father families reported a decline after treatment.

In a paper about masculinity and family work, Mason and Mason (1990) discuss men's learned behaviour being a significant contributing factor in relationship difficulties. Frosh et al. (2002), when investigating young masculinities in boys aged 11–14 years, discuss the contrast between the public peer group, where 'coolness', 'hardness' and a lack of talk about emotional issues were displayed in many boys, and the articulateness and moving stories expressed by the same boys to a sympathetic male researcher. When carrying out research interviews with 90 men (Walters, 1999), I was impressed by the warmth and concern expressed by many of the men when talking about their children, in defiance of the accepted stereotypes. With reference to parenting groups, it may be that men become polarised in their discourses in relation to female partners and that the opportunity to hear a different voice is lost in mixed-gender groups, especially where, as in most parenting groups, men are in the minority.

When co-working in a group in a CAMHS setting, I commented on how the men defied the stereotypes of not talking about their feelings. However, the group members, all fathers, felt that men only talk about their feelings when they reach 'boiling point'. They said that in the pub they chat but they don't want to 'bring the others down': nobody wants to hear 'the bad bits'.

Featherstone et al. (2007) state that male gatherings 'can easily become a forum for men to express their resentment at their partners, their limited lives, or even the world in general'. This may be more pronounced, the authors say, without a woman present. The following is an extract from the account of a fathers' group run by me and a male colleague (Staines and Walters, 2008, pp. 18–19) in a CAMHS setting:

JW: As the only woman in the group I initially wondered how comfortable this would feel but felt welcome at all times. In some instances I felt that my presence as a woman may have moderated some of the conversations that the men might have had in order not to offend their perception of me as a woman. It felt helpful sometimes to be able to put another perspective on issues such as relationships and parenting roles.

JS: In relation to working with JW I have wondered if the emotional quality of the discussions have been enhanced by having JW present. Perhaps one of my contributions as a male is a normalisation about issues that move in and out of male stereotypes and has provided a useful balance in making it safer to explore challenging areas of interpersonal relationships by rendering them not 'too unusual' (Andersen, 1992).

It is also possible that having male and female genders represented in the therapists in the group, that a certain amount of brokering (Ng, 2007) in terms of gender (as part of culture) was taking place so that an expanded range of what was able to be talked about and accepted seemed more possible.

In a recent presentation of the fathers' group to a forum of family therapists, there was an idea from a male colleague about 'all male' groups often talking using a sort of unwritten code defining the parameters of what areas could and could not be safely talked about depending on context. This same coding could also represent areas as a marker for subjects that need building up to, that could be much harder to delve into but are being acknowledged none the less.

On the one or two occasions that I facilitated the group without JW present I had a sense that the conversation seemed more coded and that I would feel less comfortable and have to take far greater risks or talk with less authority in enquiring about feelings.

Perhaps the men who kept returning for further meetings and gave such positive feedback in post-group questionnaires also preferred the talking opportunities that seemed available in this less coded and responsive gathering that respectfully included a female perspective.

Additionally it may be that a group of men invited together around the common identity of fatherhood and its struggles and talking to relative strangers with rules on confidentiality is enough to elicit the rich and diverse stories that needed to be aired, witnessed, affirmed, challenged and reflected on. It brings to mind (Frosh et al., 2002) the surprise at how well young teenage boys talked about complex interrelationships and feelings when sympathetically listened to in the respectful and bounded context of research interviews.

We wondered whether men and boys are often underestimated by others and perhaps by themselves in their ability and desire, given safe opportunities, to talk fully and meaningfully about difficult and complex emotional and relationship-based areas of their lives?

In our group we have worked hard to engage the fathers. Although we have no evidence for this having increased the likelihood of attendance, my male colleague makes initial contact with the fathers by telephone and we also invite fathers to come and meet us before attending the group

As a woman in a group of fathers, I have felt curious as the separated fathers speak of the difficulties of bringing up children on their own: not being able to take up employment or having only part-time work, and having to be both mother and father. How, I have asked, is this different from the situation of millions of women? I have felt almost impatient with the men about this. But then I have realised as they have talked that as a woman I could chat with other mothers at the school gates and network more easily in relation to activities for parents and children. I did not feel that there was a stigma attached to working part-time: quite the reverse. The model of bringing up children was there for me, but for men it is less familiar. One of the fathers in our group said, with reference to this, 'As a single father you are lost.' It seems that having a job and a workplace setting is much more important for single fathers because of the lack of social opportunities with men who are in a similar situation.

Wayne and Hari, both bringing up their children on their own as a result of separating from substance-using partners, longed to be able to work. We talked about whether it was the same as for single-parent mothers. They debated this and Hari said that it was worse for fathers because, for example at the school gates, mothers were the norm. He had additional problems because he was not from the dominant culture and so felt even more isolated.

Featherstone et al. (2007, p. 59) summarise the literature on group work with men. Rabinowitz (2005) talks of 'initial ambivalence' in men's groups before they are able to work together, although this may be true of any group. Rabinowitz stresses the need for activities and structure to reduce anxiety. Groups for offenders are often closely structured and this is necessary as there are clear aims to be achieved. The same applies to groups addressing anger management. Similarly, parenting groups such as the Webster-Stratton parenting programme have clear aims and goals which need to be identified and achieved. These are carefully measured and many of these projects are funded on the successful results. However, there is a case for groups which are less structured and more open-ended, such as the fathers' groups we run in a Child and Family Psychiatry setting (Staines and Walters, 2008). In these groups, where attendance is voluntary, we set out to provide a clear structure and to measure outcomes but have found that the men themselves prefer to set the agenda. Topics emerge to fit the needs of individuals on a week-by-week basis.

Some authors talk of the need to increase the 'emotional education' of men (Featherstone, 2007) but in our groups we have found that men's emotions are readily available when talking about their children. I also found this in my research on depression and attachment in fathers (Walters, 1999). The engagement of men in voluntary groups, however, remains a difficulty and suggests that although emotional engagement is often seen in those who attend, this is a biased sample. Nonetheless, I should add that, in our fathers' group, men are seldom seen to cry, whereas in a women's group this is more common. I do not know whether this is the case in other men's groups. However, it has been notable in my work with men how ready they are to express warm and positive feelings about their children. During one group session the men talked about how none of them were hugged by their own fathers but that they hugged their own children every day (all, incidentally, fathers of boys!). Fathers in the group can also provide great support to each other.

In the fathers' group, Wally, a lone father living with his two children, told us that his daughter had disclosed, to a teacher, abuse by her mother eighteen months previously. She had been threatened by her mother and had been too scared to tell. As the mother, who had a serious problem of sub-stance use, was no longer allowed unsupervised access to the children, the daughter had now felt safe to disclose this to her father. The disclosure was very powerful and, although a relief for the daughter, provoked great guilt in her father, who felt that he should have picked up on what was going on and protected his daughter. Another father, however, helped a great deal by reframing the situation. He said that when the father had been at home his daughter had felt safe and so had not given off signs to her father of being abused. This altered narrative helped John and reduced his guilt and feel-ings of blame.

In our fathers' group we have had several single fathers. This has been because the fathers have been widowed or, more usually, because the ex-partners have had significant problems of substance use. There is often discussion about the courts and the men's perceived bias of the system against them and in favour of the mothers.

Demitri was a father of three young children, two boys and a girl. They lived in a one-bedroomed flat and were awaiting a court hearing with regard to custody. He spoke lovingly of his children and worked very hard to be a sensitive and responsive parent. He had left home at 16 and had a poor relationship with his own father. He was keen for his children to achieve more at school than he had. His parenting was constantly being assessed in preparation for the court case and he found this very stressful in addition to caring for the children who had suffered considerable neglect and required a level of nurturing over and above the norm.

There is debate about whether or not groups for men should be structured. Clearly the way in which this is handled depends on the aims of the group and whether it is voluntary or not. There is a world of difference between a group to which there is a statutory commitment and one at which attendance is voluntary. Different ways of working with men will be appropriate for different groups and, if the work is being funded by an organisation, there is also the need for clinical work to show evidence of the aims being achieved.

It has been noted above that Moran and Ghate (2005), in a paper looking at the effectiveness of parenting support programmes, mention gender issues and the recruitment and retention of parents to services. Lloyd et al. (2003), in work evaluating the UK Sure Start project, found that specifically designed activities and a dedicated staff member were necessary to engage father in these settings. Certainly, in our fathers' group in a CAMHS setting, we ensure that the first point of contact for men to discuss the possibility of attending the group will be the male worker. However, this is not an evidence-based decision but merely a hunch that engagement might be better achieved in this way. Men will have preconceived ideas of what they are signing up for and may expect a group for fathers to have a male leader. It is interesting, nonetheless, that in my research (Walters, 1999), when I asked fathers whether they would prefer a female or male therapist, there was usually no preference, and that, where a preference was expressed, it was for a female therapist (see Chapter 5).

As with any group, the mix of participants is important. In our CAMHS group we have excluded men who have severe difficulties with, for example, substance use or management of anger and who require more specialist input. We have also found that a split has sometimes occurred between fathers who have children at primary school and those who are fathers of older children. This has meant that on occasions fathers have 'waited their turn' to speak about issues which were affecting them, rather than engaging in more of a conversation. In practice it is not always easy to overcome this, as some fathers have children who span the age range. It therefore requires skill on the part of the facilitators to ensure that common themes are addressed among the members, rather than just a series of separate issues.

We have seen in Chapter 4 how men's own parenting is highly relevant to how they parent. Certainly, an important aspect of any work with fathers, group or individual, is to think together about how they were parented and how this has influenced the way they themselves parent. I have found that this may not always be an easy conversation but that it is worth pursuing and may often produce some thoughtful dialogue, either at the time or in later sessions. The attachment and narrative paradigm, to which I have referred elsewhere, is germane here in that, through exploration of past key relationships, fathers can, in a supportive setting, be helped to see things differently and to create new or modified stories about their lives.

Our group is multiethnic and all participants speak English, although for several it is not their first language. We have not yet tried including non-English speakers but this would be possible with interpreters. In some parenting programmes interpreters are used and this is essential in terms of equal access. This may be easier in a structured programme than in a more open group.

Gosden and Kirkland (2008) write about a focus group for fathers with learning disabilities. Difficulties with recruitment to this group mean that the very small numbers involved give only a glimpse of what the issues might be. Nonetheless what emerged from their research with these fathers was an overwhelming sense of not being included. Some of them felt stigmatised by the fact that having a learning disability meant that events such as parents' evenings at school might be hard to follow. Being excluded and viewed as less important led to feelings of exclusion and isolation, which in turn led to anger and, for some, resulted in them opting out of the fathering role. However, what is striking about this work is that the themes very much echo and exacerbate the feelings of many fathers without learning disabilities. The men commented on the valuable opportunity of being able to share experiences with others.

Educational settings are a potentially great resource for working with fathers. I have mentioned one impressive project in my introduction to the book. School settings are much more normalising and less stigmatising than mental health settings and can provide excellent forums for fathers to engage, with or without their children. Projects to help fathers specifically to keep in touch with their children's learning would I am sure be of enormous importance. They might be hard to recruit to in some areas but would I think be very rewarding.

A report from Bradford on the Abiwyyat Ki Ahmiyyat project (Importance of Fatherhood project), a project set up since 2002 to engage South Asian fathers, found it hard to recruit large numbers. One reason cited was lack of confidence among the fathers. However, children have been found to be helpful in encouraging their fathers to integrate. The fathers also wanted more male workers and were discouraged by a preponderance of female staff.

The fathers in our CAMHS group gave feedback as to what they have found helpful about the group: 'Talking about problems in the open', 'Finding out you're not alone', 'Being able to discuss the situation with others and listening to others' situations', 'The group enables you to see that there are other people going through difficult times and each time you can relate to a problem it encourages you and the more you discuss the more confidence you gain', and 'I could talk about worries and be heard.'

Children and Family Centres

Children and Family Centres grew up in the 1990s in the UK as a result of the recognition that deprivation was a major factor in the lives of many children in more socially and economically deprived areas. They were linked to Sure Start projects whose remit was to embrace educational, health and family support for children in the pre-school years.

There are substantial initiatives in Children's Centres to engage fathers in group projects. A particularly successful one close to where I work in East London is a Saturday morning club for fathers and their children. Activities are organised and the sessions are well attended. There is no doubt that fathers of young children are increasingly participant in this sort of activity. There is no longer any stigma attached to men participating in leisure activities with their children, taking them to events, and so on. However, the fathers who are harder to engage are the ones who require more thought. These men may be depressed, they may be separated from their children, the relationship with the mother may not be good, and so on. Children's Centres, as with all services, have to be careful to record details of both parents where possible and to work proactively to include fathers.

Ghate, Shaw and Hazel (2000) looked at what helps and what does not help fathers in their involvement with Family Centres. They carried out a qualitative piece of research in 13 Family Centres across 7 local authorities in England and Wales during 1998–9. Interviews were held with staff and parents and fathers whether they used the centres or not. The study found that Family Centres needed a greater focus on working with men, and not just as fathers. Having an identifiable strategy was helpful. Outdoor activities and DIY were preferred. Male workers were important and there were still centres without these. However, where this was the case, it was not a complete barrier to working successfully with men. Home visits made a difference in encouraging fathers to attend Family Centres.

Family Centres are often perceived to be 'highly feminised environments'. There were negative attitudes by some female staff and female users of the centres who felt that the centre was a safe haven and could be threatened by the presence of men. There were concerns cited regarding angry men and sex offenders. Some of these attitudes made it difficult for men to attend.

The study raised the question of who the Family Centres were for. The following recommendations were made:

- reduce the level of female dominance in the centres and discourage the expression of negative attitudes towards men;
- make positive commitments to recruit fathers;
- work better at promoting centres as being for both parents and not only mothers;
- provide activities that would appeal to men, not just groups.

Proactive initiatives in Family Centres, therefore, are to provide positive images of men, to collect data on fathers in families who attend the centres in order for them to be contacted about and included in events, and to provide training for staff on how to engage and include fathers.

Conclusion

Although there are many different kinds of group projects for men, work with fathers in this area is limited. There are few research findings and views as to whether specific groups for fathers are appropriate are equivocal. Nonetheless, there is a need for more research in this area and a strong evaluation of existing projects.

Practice points

- It can be difficult to set up groups for men. Consider carefully your aims and whether there is a rationale for what you are hoping to do. Is it what the population you are working with want?
- Recruitment and engagement is demanding work and best achieved by a designated male worker.
- Consider your goals and whether these will be best achieved by a structured format or a more open-ended meeting.

- Meet potential participants formally beforehand. Group members who have specific problems with mental health, substance use or management of anger, or who cannot keep boundaries in this setting, may not be suitable unless your group is addressing these specific problem areas.

DOMESTIC VIOLENCE AND FATHERS IN PRISON

This chapter looks at working with domestic violence and also with families where the father is in prison. These areas can be particularly challenging and often fall to those working in social care services or inner-city clinical practices.

Domestic violence and men

Featherstone (2009) points out that, despite there being information on the prevalence of men-to-women domestic violence, there is little in the way of reliable research to say how much domestic violence is carried out by fathers. Workers in the child protection field are very familiar with children who have experienced violence and abuse from parents. A UK study (Cawson et al., 2000) for the NSPCC, quoted by Featherstone, found that fathers were responsible for 40 per cent of the physical abuse suffered by children and mothers 49 per cent. Sexual abuse was carried out by only 1 per cent of fathers or stepfathers but just under 20 per cent of the sample said that they had been afraid of their father or stepfather in childhood.

I almost invariably ask about the father if he is absent from my consultations. It always produces useful information and the mother is usually willing to say something, even if the topic seems sensitive. Talking about the father can then involve the children and their views, and inevitably the information is relevant and will create a context for further discussion of the children's problems. If talking about a father who has, for example, been violent causes too much upset, it may at times be better to see the mother alone for her to give details. However, for children to acknowledge the upset in themselves and their parent can often be helpful and can be part of the work at a later stage.

Maureen's father was violent to her mother and also to her and her sib-lings throughout Maureen's childhood. He finally separated from her mother, although not until Maureen had left home. She subsequently went on to have several children with different men, all of whom were physi-cally violent to her. She began to use drugs and then lost the care of her children.

There is no doubt that most forms of conflict between parents will upset the children. The extent of the conflict, including whether it is verbal and/or physical, occasional or repeated, will of course be rel-evant in terms of the damage that is inflicted on the children. Some children witness more than one partner being violent to their parent, usually the mother.

Jagdish told me that he saw his mother's head being smashed against a window pane by her second partner. He came to the clinic referred for violent behaviour at home. He had started secondary school and much of his life had been lived with violent exchanges between his mother and two different men. He and his mother had not previously discussed the violence so openly, in her case because she had felt ashamed and in his case because he had tried to forget it. Both were traumatised. The aim of therapy was to help both to form a different narrative around the events. This would enable Jagdish's mother to understand that she had been a victim of the violence and that she had done well eventually to ask the men to leave in order to protect herself and the children. For Jagdish the narrative was around the reasons why his father had been violent and had had to go, allowing him to develop an understanding of his father's own history and harsh upbringing and also trying to give him some hope of himself as a young male growing up and to elicit some positive stories of fathering.

Sometimes a parent, usually the mother, will say that the children did not witness the violence but that they may have heard argu-ments. This is often dubious as, when disputes are in progress, it is unlikely that those involved will be fully aware of what is going on around them. It is therefore wise always to assume that a child has seen or heard more than has been stated. Young children may draw or play out some of the scenes they have witnessed and other may be able to talk if facilitated.

Arthur and Kylie were separating. There had been a lot of arguments. Their 12-year- old daughter was saying that she wanted to die. An older child had dropped out of school. The parents were happy for their daughter to be seen on her own but were not keen to work as a family. They said that they did not want their 6-year-old son to be involved because he was not aware of what was happening and his daily life was not affected.

Much has been written about parental conflict and its effects on children. Witnessing aggression can have deleterious effects. Jenkins (2000) points out that researchers previously subscribed to a stress model relationship whereby marital disharmony was related to child psychopathology. She develops this idea to examine emotional regulation in children in homes where stress is high and who show difficulties in regulating negative affect. In an unusual study, Jenkins looked at the interactions with their peers of 71 children aged between four and eight in Canada. As well as the usual ratings by teachers and parents, she also obtained ratings by peers of behaviour. She found that anger-based marital conflict was found to be strongly associated with ratings by teachers, parents and peers of aggression. Sadly, however, the author points out that data from fathers were not collected and, owing to limited resources, 'it was necessary to rely on mothers' judgements of fathers' anger-based conflict as the measure of fathers' behaviour (p. 732).

Similarly, Jaffee et al. (2003), in a UK study, used data from an epidemiological sample of 1,116 five-year-olds and their parents. They found that where fathers have high levels of antisocial behaviour and live at home, the children are at great risk of conduct problems, and that children do not always benefit from growing up with two parents if one is antisocial. The focus should be on the behaviour of the people raising the children, rather than on having two parents. The authors sensibly conclude that 'marriage may not be the answer to the problems faced by some children living in single-parent families unless their fathers can become reliable sources of emotional and economic support'(p. 109).

The effects of marital discord on young adults has been researched by Amato and Afifi (2006). Lower subjective well-being and poorer-quality parent–child relationships were found for those who had been with parents in high-conflict marriages. Where conflict had been low, no differences were reported by the offspring of divorced or non-divorced couples regarding 'feeling caught'.

Janice, aged 11, was referred by her school for truanting. She lived with her mother, stepfather and two younger siblings, the younger of whom was a half-sibling. Janice had recently been in a fight with a boy and had been injured seriously enough to need a stay in hospital.

Janice had grown up until the age of six with her father who was violent to her mother. Her mother described desperate scenes when her head had been smashed against a wall by her former partner. Janice had witnessed these scenes but they had never been talked about. There was now no contact with Janice's father.

Through several sessions with mother and daughter where Janice could try and piece together some of the memories and terrible fear she felt when her father attacked her mother, some understanding of her own attraction to violence developed. She seemed to have a better understanding of the value of her stepfather and his more passive approach to her and her mother. Unfortunately, Janice and her mother did not continue treatment at the point where the stepfather was invited to attend appointments.

Talking directly about risk and helping fathers to develop responsibility for their behaviour and the safety of others is discussed by Cooper and Vetere (2005), who have worked extensively with families where domestic violence has occurred. If fathers are not present they are made visible by thinking about them, writing about them and gaining different viewpoints about them. The violence often needs to be contextualised in a picture of the father's own life and upbringing. It is, for example, known that harsh physical punishment in childhood is related to more intimate partner violence in adult life (Swinford et al., 2000). 'Legacies of harm' are explored (Vetere and Cooper, 2006) but the authors are also looking for stories of 'resilience, support and strength'. The authors go on to talk of how they often find that men need to be 'educated/persuaded of their relevance to their children'. They also emphasise through a case illustration how little support there is for men who are concerned about their behaviour. Men may keep their own histories of abuse to themselves and listening to these stories of violence and neglect for the first time can be a powerful intervention. It is difficult to know how best to elicit these stories, particularly in men who do not attend healthcare settings. But all health workers should be aware of this aspect and create opportunities for men to talk if it seems necessary. Where there has been severe harm or abuse, it may be that workers need to refer on to more specialist teams if the man is in agreement with this.

Tom had custody of his two boys. The older one was bullying the younger one and Tom felt very angry about it. However, the older boy had experienced violence from his mother who had had long-standing problems with substance use. Tom himself had left home at 15 and, until the idea that he had had to bring himself up from an unusually early age was raised, he had not reflected on this. He talked about it in the group and began to realise that, as a result of his own experiences, he was expecting a lot of his son, who was entering adolescence. He decided to talk calmly with his son about the bullying of the younger brother, explaining how it might make the little boy feel and linking it with his son's experiences of abuse from his mother. The bullying reduced immediately and Tom was able to understand how this calmer approach was more effective than a punitive one.

A professional couple sought help regarding the challenging behaviour of their teenage daughter. After two interviews with the family and one with the daughter alone, it was revealed by the daughter's older brother that the father had hit her. The clinician, who was very experienced, decided not to report this immediately but to give the father a stern warning about the consequences of his behaviour. This was in the context of understanding the immense pressures he felt himself to be under as a result of his daughter's behaviour and other family stresses, such as the serious illness of his sister, whose husband had left her with three children. The father was asked who else knew that he had hit his daughter. The answer was no one and it was suggested that a trusted friend or relative could be brought into the picture and consulted when there was a potential risk of violence. The power of someone outside the family knowing about the violence is great and is often a very effective therapeutic intervention. In this case, the father felt supported, the dynamics in his relationship with his daughter changed and the violence ceased.

Hardesty et al. (2008) looked at coparenting relationships for 25 divorced mothers who had experienced violence during their marriage. Keeping parental and spousal roles differentiated or separate was found to be central to coparenting dynamics. The authors suggest that interventions can be more appropriately matched by understanding the variations in coparenting relationships following divorce.

We must not forget the increasing recognition that men can also be the victims of abuse (Holden and Barker, 2004) and must not always assume that they are the perpetrators. Fathers need support in this area, particularly because the popular image is of violent men and not women. In fact, there is increasing evidence of women's violence. Men may be victimised by women in this way and it can be hard to prove.

Fathers and child protection

Featherstone, in a workshop in April 2008 (Gender and Child Welfare Network Workshop, McGill University), is reported as noting the important issue of the involvement of fathers in children's lives not being seen as inherently good. Men can use contact to control women, and often women are responsible for negotiating contact between fathers and children. In this meeting Featherstone is reported as stressing the need for an understanding of fatherhood, acknowledging the complexities inherent in that role. However, where fathers are a negative influence in the family, this does not mean that they should be excluded from services. In fact, it underlines the need for services to work with these men.

Featherstone (2009) also makes the important point that 'very few studies of the families of the children who come into contact with social services departments have focused on fathers. It would appear from the very limited evidence we have that non-resident fathers and father figures are disproportionately represented on social work caseloads when compared with the wider population' (Roskill et al., 2008, p. 36). Ryan (2006), looking at the experiences of fathers involved in Social Services departments, found that men had multiple problems with unemployment and mental and physical health difficulties and that there were high levels of conflict between the men and women. Many had suffered neglect in their own childhoods. Interestingly, it was found by Egan-Sage and Carpenter (1999) that the youngest and oldest fathers had more children on the register.

Featherstone (2003) looks at the changing constructions of fathers in the child protection system where 'notions of threat ... appear more dominant as a theme' (p. 239). She talks of themes of fathers as risks or resources, the possibility of dialogues moving beyond this polarised thinking, and developing 'practices which do justice to the complexities of their [fathers'] lives and relationships'.

Fathers often have a negative perception of the social care system. Where they are less involved with their families, this can be exacerbated by the intervention of professionals. There is therefore a need for professionals to make extra efforts to involve fathers. Unfortunately, workers can feel threatened by fathers and they will need support from experienced supervisors. Separated fathers can be particularly vulnerable in the planning process and some mothers will inevitably block contact. Careful assessments must be made of where contact with fathers is likely to be productive and where not. The best interests of the child are obviously paramount.

I was surprised, following a workshop in early 2009 which I had presented with my colleague John Staines on working with separated fathers, that two young social workers approached us afterwards and said how seldom they had thought about inviting fathers to family meetings. David Bartlett (2008), from the Fatherhood Institute, makes recommendations following comments on Lord Laming's review on safeguarding. Bartlett states that there are crucial issues regarding engaging with fathers where there are child protection concerns. These are not being adequately handled in some local authorities. Bartlett states, 'If the risks and protective factors of men in a child's family are not assessed effectively then the child is likely to be placed at greater risk'. The recommendations are worth looking at in detail. Bartlett stresses that there is a lot of evidence regarding the importance of effective engagement with abusive fathers.

The Fatherhood Institute recommends gender-inclusive local strategies; policies for social care services which set out how to involve fathers, including those who are non-resident; attendance of fathers at planning meetings concerning children to be monitored; staff training with regard to working with fathers; staff working with families to explore children's views about their father or a father figure; and, finally, effective support and supervisory structures to be put in place where there are fears about violence.

In the same vein the Family Rights Group (2006, 2008) has pointed out the shortfall in social care services for fathers. They also point out that practitioners are lacking practical help and information. The FRG calls for social workers to be trained in dealing with fathers. From their findings, the FRG have developed courses for social care workers on working with fathers. This is a specialist area of work. Fathers themselves have joined as trainers. A specific area of research is that of working with fathers who are violent in the home. Bartlett states that data from an NSPCC project found that a fifth of their sample of children were afraid of their fathers. Fear of the father (or any other parental figure) may not be obvious but, where it is picked up, it should be recognised under the category of emotional abuse.

In addition, child protection conferences need to take into account the difficulties that fathers may have in attending and should ensure that all forms requesting information on children should specify 'father and mother' and not just 'parent'. Staff should always try to involve fathers, except where the situation seems to be unsafe or where the father does not have parental responsibility and the mother refuses to allow social care agencies to involve him (where the work is not statutory). Records must have the birth father's details, and those of any other father figure, their involvement in the child's life, and whether they have parental responsibility. Planning meetings should always include the fathers. Attempts should be made to engage with non-resident fathers. Where there are care proceedings, letters should be sent to the fathers as well as the mothers, inviting them to the meetings. The fathers' views should always be given due consideration.

Importantly, it is recommended that complex cases should be given to experienced social workers and that, where men are violent or threatening, effective structures for supervision and safety should be put in place.

In sum, 'all policies impacting upon children's or adult services should recognise men in their fathering role and the importance of engaging fathers as well as mothers' (Roskill et al., 2008, p. 8).

The FRG stresses the need for early intervention rather than, as they say often happens, allowing the situation where fathers ask for help from Social Care services and there is no response until there is a crisis. This does, however, reflect to some extent the pressure on services: as a result of time constraints, work with fathers who are hard to engage can be seen as almost peripheral and easy to eliminate.

Further recommendations are parenting groups and courses that welcome fathers, and supervised contact centres that are open at weekends. More programmes for violent and abusive fathers are called for. Other measures recommended are family advocacy, family group conferences and family mediation.

Some fathers do not know that their children have been taken into care or that children's services are involved. When they do and when they want to be involved, they do not know how to ask for help. Some helplines can be useful for engaging fathers, particularly in these situations, but dedicated time and money needs to be devoted to these services to make them effective and useful.

Fathers in prison

More than 125,000 children are affected annually by parents going into prison (Fatherhood Institute, 2006). Not infrequently in our work we meet with children whose fathers are in prison. This can inevitably raise a number of issues, including what the children have been told, what they actually know, the stigma, contact, poverty, and so on. Reoffending rates drop by up to six times if fathers stay in touch with their families. Their children are less likely to commit crimes.

Day (2005) edited an issue of Fathering in which there were several accounts of research with men imprisoned in the US and the UK.

In particular, they placed emphasis in their research upon the reintegration into family life of men coming out of prison and the relationship between the reintegration and reoffending rates. However, there are no standard arrangements for imprisoned fathers to attend the birth of their child, many prisons have no visitors' centre, and thousands of prisoners are held far from home. Also, there is often no officer with responsibility for dealing with family matters, and information about parenthood is not routinely recorded. Half of young fathers receive no visits from their children, and many sons go on to be convicted. In Young Offender Institutions 25 per cent of men are shortly to become fathers.

In the UK there has been a 43 per cent increase in the prison population since 1993 (Office for National Statistics, 2005). Day reports that successful reintegration into family life is associated with lower rates of rearrest and incarceration (recidivism). Where this does not work, there can be a greater financial burden on families, problems with the transmission of infectious diseases (HIV, Hepatitis C, TB), substance use, rapid reoffending, and children growing up in poverty.

Children of fathers in prison suffer many problems, including emotional difficulties and school-related difficulties such as poor academic performance (reviewed by Hagan and Dinovitzer, 1999). Murray and Farrington (2008) report on the effects of parental imprisonment on boys' internalising problems. The researchers using the Cambridge Study in Delinquent Development compared boys separated as a result of parental imprisonment during the first 10 years of life with four other groups – those who had no separation, those separated through hospitalisation or death, those separated as a result of parental disharmony, and those whose parents were imprisoned prior to their birth. Measures were made of individual, parenting and family risk factors for internalising problems when the boys were aged 8 to 11. They found that separation as a result of parental imprisonment predicted boys' internalising problems and antisocial problems from age 14 to 48, suggesting that these effects are long term.

There are few transitional programmes for men who are trying to reintegrate into families. However, Petersilia (2003) states that most prisoners are inside short term (average 29 months), most are young (average age 26), and most will attempt to reconnect with partners and children. Murray (2002), in a paper written for Action for Prisoners' Families, talks about how fathers in prison miss their children acutely and also relates the suicide rate to this. Murray states that children who have a father in prison have increased problems with depression and anxiety, school performance and delinquency, and are at risk of being in prison themselves later in their lives. He does, however, also point out that some children can of course flourish when violent or uncaring parents are removed, and it is important to keep this in mind. Variables in relation to how children are affected are the age of the children, their care following incarceration, what they are told about it and the length of time in prison and separation. It is interesting to consider, much as in children of divorced parents, how much the effects are due to the actual imprisonment and how much they are due to what went before in terms of the children's lives. Often these children will have been brought up in poor neighbourhoods and will have suffered social stigma and financial deprivation. Murray states that one third of children are told nothing about where their father is and another third are not told the truth. What children are told can depend on their age and cognitive ability but he rightly states that lack of knowledge can be damaging, especially if they discover the truth from another source, in which case a sense of betrayal can result. Many children do, however, have regular contact with their father in prison and this may be through visits, letters or telephone calls. Distance from the prison is a relevant factor in relation to visits, and the attitude of the partner is also an important variable. There is growing awareness of how important it is for fathers to be in contact with their children while in prison, and some prisons have developed strategies to help with this. These include running parenting courses. The need for teachers to be aware of those children whose father is in prison and how to deal with this is raised by Murray.

The following family is one that did not return to the clinic.

A mother attended the clinic with her two young boys. Their father was in prison but, before release, a decision as to whether he should be deported had to be made. The mother had a new partner who had two children, and the boys had not been taken to see their father for several months. They were displaying some difficult behaviour at school. It seemed that the contact with the father had been lost early on, possibly as a result of the mother's ambivalence and the uncertainty surrounding the children's father's possible deportation. However, if contact had been facilitated and maintained, it is possible that this might have influenced the decisions regarding his future.

A father's good relationship with the child's mother is critical in maintaining access to the children (Clarke et al., 2005). There can be beneficial effects on government budgets, which are greatly reduced by the better reintegration into family life of ex-prisoners. Potentially there is the lower cost of prison facilities, and less family poverty as a result of rehabilitative programmes but there are considerable methodological issues involved in gaining access to prisoners for research. Safety is also another issue. Some interviewers work in pairs. Where guards were present, this was anecdotally said to 'dampen' the interview' (Day, 2005). It would be understandable if men were less inclined to display emotion when being interviewed in the presence of an official. Systematic recruitment to projects can often be difficult as a result of various prison regulations. Sometimes researchers are also unsure how projects have been presented by the guards. A small proportion of men interviewed pretended that they were fathers when in fact they were not. Clarke et al. (2005) report that in Britain men's parental status is not routinely checked on admission to prison. This seems to be an extremely shocking omission. It was felt by Day (2005) that being on site in the prison for some weeks would be a good way to build trust with both staff and inmates.

Interviews with prisoners' partners were often difficult to instigate (Day, 2005). This sometimes indicated discrepancies between the ideals of the men and the women's vision of the return to family life. Men sometimes believed that they would have access whereas the women were less willing than the men realised. There was also a tendency for men to rate themselves as 'good' fathers despite some evidence to the contrary.

Follow-up interviews post-release proved difficult, although the US system of more coordination with the prison prior to and after release than in the UK facilitated this aspect.

Dyer (2005) researched how being in prison affected the fathers' identity as fathers. Fathers cannot enact fathering roles while in prison. There are some innovative projects in which fathers are enabled to keep closer contact with their children in various ways, such as writing in journals. However, more research is necessary in this area. It is pointed out by Clarke et al. (2005, p. 223) how 'the usual domains of responsible or active fatherhood' (i.e. financial support and active emotional and physical care) are almost impossible to fulfil when the father is incarcerated. The key interpersonal relationship for the father in prison is with the mother, whose mediating influence between the father and children is crucial. This echoes my research on clinic attendance by fathers (Walters et al., 2001) which suggests that relationships between parents affect attendance rates of fathers at appointments. Where the partner relationship is poor, the links between the father and services can obviously be restricted.

Clarke et al. (2005) point out that fathers are, of course, not a homogeneous group. They discovered 'great variability both in attitudes and behaviour' (p. 238). There are many barriers to fathering roles from a prison context, and individuals in such settings are stigmatised by society. Fathers may be able to write and receive letters, or receive telephone calls or visits, but for many this would entail a lot of emotional effort. Visits are made at prescribed times and may seem artificial. For some fathers it may even feel easier to cut themselves off from their children than to acknowledge the pain that separation entails.

Practical considerations are important. It may also be difficult for families with several children to visit together where there are very young children and perhaps older ones in the same family. Simply travelling to the prison or arranging childcare may present problems.

In Clarke's sample the 43 men, whose ages ranged from 23 to 48, not surprisingly had complex relationship histories and the majority had not been married to their children's mother. Good relationships with the children's mother was crucial for maintaining access to the children. Arditti et al. (2005) confirm this from interviews with 51 imprisoned fathers in the US which demonstrated how men were entirely dependent on mothers or caregivers for contact with their children. Many men felt powerless in this situation. However, the authors point out that it is not always clear whether contact is beneficial: in some instances it may not be so. Contact, both while in prison and on release, needs to be beneficial to both father and family. In the paper by Arditti et al., entitled 'It's been hard to be a father', they recommend narrative therapy for the imprisoned men whereby they can deconstruct this notion and reconstruct the narrative to less impoverishing themes. This can be done through journals and letters as well as through therapeutic meetings.

Keith's father was in prison. He had been separated from the family for several years following drug use and domestic violence witnessed by Keith. At first Keith's mother did not tell him that his father has been imprisoned but then the father, via his lawyers, requested visits from the children. Keith's mother did not want him to see his father but wondered whether letters should be allowed.

Bahr et al. (2005) echo the ideas above regarding quality of contact with the child's mother being closely related to outcomes when leaving prison. Bahr states that the family network and close relationships are also important. The criminal trajectory is harder to change where there are conflicted family relationships. Also of importance are the peer group and drugs. These influences can be negative and can impact on the potential for rehabilitation. Stability of housing is a further important factor, although presumably getting away from an area where there have been negative influences could help.

Clarke et al. (2005) recommend that parental status be recorded routinely for prisoners. This would then create the potential for maintaining family relationships and enhancing resettlement. Roy and Dyson (2005) echo Clarke's findings and state that 'in the creation of effective family policies, programmes that promote supportive interpersonal ties may actually deter recidivism and contribute to a new ethos of rehabilitation' (p. 307).

Bahr et al. (2005) recommend that parent–child contact be encouraged, that families be supported, that employment and training opportunities be increased and that more treatment for drug use be implemented.

Harem was nine when he was referred for help with outbursts at school and at home. His father had gone to prison when Harem was two and was no longer in contact. The outbursts started when Harem's stepfather, who had been with his mother for four years, was also imprisoned for several years. Harem was close to his stepfather and the loss hit him very badly. He did not understand why his stepfather had gone to prison.

Exploration of Harem's story revealed that his mother had held back a lot of the truth about his stepfather but that she herself was still shocked by the harsh sentence. Some of the clinical work involved helping her to come to terms with what had happened. This enabled her to be more open with Harem about his stepfather. Arrangements were made for Harem to pay regular visits to his stepfather in prison. Over several months Harem became more settled emotionally, although it seemed that it would take a long time for him to process the story of both his fathers and essentially how he felt let down by them.

Children in this situation often have to cope with family shame about what has happened. This can be far-reaching as it affects not only the immediate family but also means that the children have to cope with the fact that people in the neighbourhood and their peers at school are aware of the situation. It is important to stick to the truth as far as possible because rumours abound and stories become exaggerated. Children can suffer greatly in this situation, especially as a result of peer behaviour.

A teenage boy in a very difficult family, where the father had left and the older brother was in prison, was said by the social worker to be 'carrying the male violence for the family'. The mother was worried that he would turn out to be the same as his father and brother.

Smith and Farrington (2004) researched antisocial behaviour and parenting across generations. They studied data on 411 males from inner London, their female partners, their parents and their children. They found that males who were poorly supervised as children were themselves poor supervisors as fathers. The authors state that having a criminal father predicts the likelihood of delinquency, independent of other strong risk factors which may be poor school performance, a disruptive family and poor parenting. Studies, such as those by Farrington (2000) (cited in Smith and Farrington, 2004), found that having a criminal father almost doubled the risk of a son being convicted. They found that there is a strong concentration in families. Intergenerational links hypothesised are as might be expected: biopsychosocial influences such as continuities in deprived environments, genetic factors, partner and peer selection, and parenting factors. Education and schools will also have a strong influence in relation to these factors. Schools can, for example, influence achievement and peer relationships, and can, to varying degrees, help with learning difficulties. There is enormous variation in inner-city schools between those that identify difficulties early on and provide appropriate support and those that, for many reasons, do not. Many primary schools are now linked in to parenting programmes, as children are arriving at school with poor social and learning skills associated with poor parenting. For example, in Hackney, an inner London borough, there is an active Early Intervention Parenting Project focused on families with a child aged 3 to 8 years linked to the Parenting Institute. An associated programme (SPOKES) emphasises parenting in the context of improving literacy in young children. However, there is a paucity of studies on the specific influence of fathers' parenting on child behaviour.

It was found by Smith and Farrington, however, that although some continuity across generations was suggested, there were no significant findings for child conduct difficulties. Links with having a convicted grandfather or grandmother were 'somewhat elevated' (2004, p. 242) but not significant.

Clinically it can be hard to work with children whose fathers are in prison and the dilemmas presented are not simple.

A young child was referred because of difficult behaviour at school. His father was in prison serving a long sentence. He did not understand where his father was or what it meant. His mother had not talked to him about it. The stigma for the family in their community was also a very negative factor. This was a dilemma for the clinician and consideration was given to how this child might be given some relevant information to help him to have a story about his father, rather than the issue being completely avoided. This enabled the mother to be more comfortable in the parenting of her son.

The narrative around this child's father needed to be appropriate for his age. This created further dilemmas in that there were several children in the family and each understood different aspects of what had happened. However, it was the referred child who appeared to be struggling most, although it could be said that this was more apparent as a result of his behaviour and that perhaps the others worried in other ways.

Narratives and stories about our families can and do change throughout life and this boy needed a story which was appropriate at that time but which could be adapted as he grew older and understood more.

Conclusion

Working with families where the father is or has been violent requires special training and support. Similarly, where fathers are in prison, workers need to be aware of the specialist help available to families to enable them to maintain contact, if that is what is wanted, and to provide support for the families with regard to the stigma.

Practice points

- Men's own stories of being victims of violence and neglect should be listened to.
- Where a father is seeking help for his behaviour, support should be provided or he should be referred on to an appropriate agency. It can be suggested that the father think of a third party outside the family setting who can be made aware of the risk of violence.
- The parental status of men in prison should be routinely documented.

- Reoffending rates are reduced if men are in contact with their families. Children are less likely to offend if family contact is maximised. Family liaison workers are needed to facilitate contact where it is thought to be helpful.
- Employment and training opportunities for fathers in prison are needed so that rehabilitation is facilitated.

ENDNOTE

The topic of working with fathers potentially embraces vast areas of research and literature. In this book I have often been only touching on ideas that deserve more space, attention and thought. However, the main point of the book is to emphasise how important it is to keep fathers in mind in our work with children and families. I have tried through many case examples to demonstrate how we can keep fathers in mind and work with them when available or how to work without them if they are not there. I hope that I have managed to achieve this to some extent and have been able to promote thought with regard to fathers, whether present in the family or absent. There is no doubt that that life in the twenty-first century is inevitably different from that for previous generations and that roles have changed, with fathers playing a bigger part in domains previously inhabited by women. However, fathers are still often neglected in research, not always thought of in family work, and in many cases seen as peripheral. I have something of a passion for this topic, as I hope I have managed to convey, but feel exasperated at times at how fathers can still be ignored.

I have illustrated through research findings and case examples some of the salient points about fathers and how we might try to work with them. The research findings are often equivocal and we all have narratives or stories from our own lives which shape our beliefs. It is impossible to generalise about fathers. At a teaching session about fathers, when participants were asked for words that sprang to mind regarding fathers the following were suggested: angry, loving, kind, disciplinarian, waste of space, absent, firm, playful, isolated, reticent, over the top, old-fashioned, cool, useless, sad, crazy, funny, soft, and so on. The list is endless and it is hard to be clear about fathers and their roles because they are so diverse.

We have seen how good relationships between partners foster better parent–child relationships. Fathers who are vulnerable are those who have conflictual relationships, poor mental health, poor experiences of being parented, in low- paid jobs or unemployed. These factors may all be interlinked. Unfortunately these fathers may also be the group who are least likely to seek help and are therefore hard to reach. Father contact with children may not always be the best thing, particularly with regard to those who have been involved in crime or violence. However, they may still need support and supervised contact with children, and services need to address ways of achieving this where appropriate. Indeed, it may be part of a rehabilitative programme. Programmes are needed for these fathers which address their mental health, job status, substance use or the fact that they are separated or divorced. Young fathers often require support with housing.

At a work team meeting recently, a colleague commented that she felt that we were seeing more fathers in the clinic than had previously been the case, in couples anyway. I think that this is true, although I worry more about the ones who do not come, who are hard to reach, as I think they are the ones who might be harder to work with but with whom some work might make a real difference.

Using an attachment and narrative framework exploration of fathers' own histories with their fathers is an important aspect of work that may be done clinically with fathers alone or with their families. Poor attachments and unspoken and unexplored losses can be at the root of many mental health problems and, for men espe-cially, listening to them and helping them to communicate, articulate and reframe some of these feelings in a sensitive setting can be ground-breaking in enabling relationships to change.

I have pointed out how neglected fathers remain in research. I think the idea still prevails that men are hard to engage, both in services and research. I hope I have managed to convey how this is often simply not the case. The more that fathers are kept in mind, the easier it will become to engage them, even those who are harder to reach. It is simply not good enough for fathers, present or absent, to be ignored by those working with children in any area, be it research, mental health, social care, education or family centres. In work in adult services, such as mental health and prison services, data on parental status must routinely be collected and the implications taken seriously. Whether positively or negatively, fathers are part of children's lives (indeed all our lives), even if only in their thoughts, and they need to be kept firmly in mind. "In his own mind, no child is 'without a father'" (Kraemer, 2005) and neither should any child be without a father in our minds.

REFERENCES

Abidin, R. R., Jenkins, C. L. & McGaughey, M. C. (1992) 'The relationship of early family variables to children's subsequent behavioral adjustment', *Journal of Clinical Child Psychology*, 21(1), 60–69.

Abiwiyyat Ki Ahmiyyat (Importance of Fatherhood) (2002–) *Project Case Study (Muslim Fathers): Helping South Asian Men Embrace Their Role as Fathers*, http://www.fatherhoodinstitute.org/index.php?id=8&cID=654

Addis, M. & Mahalik, J. (2003) 'Men, masculinity, and the contexts of help seeking', *American Psychologist*, 58, 5–14.

Agras, S. A., Bryson, M. A., Hammer, L. D. & Kraemer, H. C. (2007) 'Childhood risk factors for thin body preoccupation and social pressure to be thin', *Journal of the American Academy of Child and Adolescent Psychiatry*, 46, 171–178.

Ainsworth, M., Blehar, M., Waters, E. & Wall, S. (1978) *Patterns of Attachment: A Psychological Study of the Strange Situation*. Hillsdale, NJ: Lawrence Erlbaum.

Allan, G. & Crow, G. (2001) *Families, Households and Society*. Basingstoke: Palgrave.

Allen, J. G. & Fonagy, P. (eds) (2006) *Handbook of Mentalization-Based Treatment*. Chichester: John Wiley.

Amato, P. (1994) 'Father–child relations, mother–child relations, and off-spring psychological well-being in early adulthood', *Journal of Marriage and the Family*, 56, 1031–1042.

Amato, P. & Afifi, T. (2006) 'Feeling caught between parents: Long-term consequences for parent–child relationships and psychological well-being', *Journal of Marriage and Family*, 68, 222–235.

Amato, P. R. & Gilbreth, J. G. (1999), 'Non-resident fathers and children's well-being: A meta-analysis', *Journal of Marriage and the Family*, 61, 557–573.

Andersen, T. (1992) 'Reflections on reflecting with families', in S. McNamee & K. J. Gergen (eds), *Therapy as Social Construction*. London: Sage.

Apfel, R. J. & Handel, M. H. (1993), 'Fathers with major mental illness: An ignored population', in *Madness and Loss of Motherhood: Sexuality, Reproduction and Long-term Mental Illness*. Washington, DC & London: American Psychiatric Press Inc.

Arditti, J. A., Smock, S. & Parkman, T. (2005) 'It's been hard to be a father: A qualitative exploration of incarcerated fatherhood', *Fathering*, 3, 267–288.

Aries, P. (1962) *Centuries of Childhood*. New York: Vintage.

Atkins, R. & Lansky, M. (1986) 'The father in family therapy: Psychoanalytic perspectives', in Lamb (ed.), *The Father's Role.*

Atkinson, A. K. & Rickel, A. U. (1984) 'Postpartum depression in primiparous parents', *Journal of Abnormal Psychology*, 93, 115–119.

Auster, P. (1988) *The Invention of Solitude.* London: Faber.

Bagner, D. & Eyberg, S. M. (2003) 'Father involvement in parent training: When does it matter?', *Journal of Clinical Child and Adolescent Psychology*, 32, 599–605.

Bahr, S. J., Harker Armstrong, A., Guild Gibbs, B., Harris, P. E. & Fisher, J. K. (2005) 'The reentry process: How parolees adjust to release from prison', *Fathering*, 3, 267–288.

Bailey, W. T. (1991) 'Fathers' involvement in their children's healthcare', *Journal of Genetic Psychology*, 152(3), 289–293.

Ballard, C. G., Davis, R., Cullen, P. C., Mohan, R. N. & Dean, C. (1994) 'Prevalence of postnatal psychiatric morbidity in mothers and fathers', *British Journal of Psychiatry*, 164, 782–788.

Barnett, R. C., Marshall, N. L. & Pleck, J. H. (1992) 'Men's multiple roles and their relationship to men's psychological distress', *Journal of Marriage and the Family*, 54, 358–367.

Barrett, H. & Tasker, F. (2002) 'Gay fathers and their children: What we know and what we need to know', *Lesbian and Gay Psychology Review*, 3, 3–10.

Bartholomew, K. (1990) 'Avoidance of intimacy: An attachment perspective', *Journal of Social and Personal Relationships*, 7, 147–178.

Bartholomew, K. & Horowitz, L. M. (1991) 'Attachment styles among young adults: A test of a four category model', *Journal of Personality and Social Psychology*, 61, 226–244.

Bartlett, D. (2008) Comments for Lord Laming's *Review on Safeguarding.* London: Fatherhood Institute, 5 December.

Beail, N. (ed.) (1982) *Fathers: Psychological Perspectives.* London: Junction Books.

Bell, B. G. & Belsky, J. (2007) 'Parenting and childrens' cardiovascular functioning', *Child: Care, health and development*, 24, 194–203.

Belsky, J. (1984) 'The determinants of parenting: A process model', *Child Development*, 55, 83–96.

Belsky, J. (1993) 'Promoting father involvement – An analysis and critique: Comment on Silverstein', *Journal of Family Psychology*, 7, 3.

Belsky, J., Youngblade, L., Rovine, M. & Volling, B. (1991) 'Patterns of marital change and parent–child interaction', *Journal of Marriage and the Family*, 53, 487–498.

Bennun, I. (1989) 'Perceptions of the therapist in family therapy', *Journal of Family Therapy*, 11, 243–255.

Benoit, D. & Parker, K. (1994) 'Stability and transmission of attachment across three generations', *Child Development*, 65, 1444–1456.

Berg, B. & Rosenblum, N. (1977) 'Fathers in family therapy: A survey of family therapists', *Journal of Marriage and Family Counselling*, 3, 85–91.

Berlyn, C., Wise, S. & Soriano, G. (2008) *Engaging fathers in child and family services. Participation, perceptions and good practice.* Occasional Paper No. 22. National Evaluation Consortium. Department of Families, Housing, Community Services and Indigenous Affairs. Canberra.

Berman, P. W. & Pedersen, F. A. (1987) *Men's Transitions to Parenthood.* Hove and London: Lawrence Erlbaum.

Bielawska-Batorowicz, E. & Kossakowska-Petrycka, K. (2006) 'Depressive mood in men after the birth of their offspring in relation to a partner's depression, social support, father's personality and prenatal expectations', *Journal of Reproductive and Infant Psychology*, 24, 21–29.

Bifulco, A. & Moran, P. (1998) *Wednesday's Child.* London & New York: Routledge.

Bilker, L. (1993) 'Male or female therapists for eating-disordered adolescents: Guidelines suggested by research and practice', *Adolescence*, 28(110), 393–422.

Biringen, Z. (1994) 'Attachment theory and research: Application to clinical practice', *American Journal of Orthopsychiatry*, 64(3), 404–420.

Blackie, S. & Clark, D. (1987) 'Men in marriage counselling', in C. Lewis (ed.), *Reassessing Fatherhood: New Observations on Fathers and Modern Families.* London: Sage.

Blazer, D. G., Kessler, R. C., McGonagle, K. A. & Swartz, M. S. (1994), 'The prevalence and distribution of major depression in a national community sample: The National Comorbidity Survey', *American Journal of Psychiatry*, 151, 979–986.

Blendis, J. (1982) 'Men's experiences of their own fathers', in Beail (ed.), *Fathers: Psychological Perspectives.*

Bogels, S. & Phares, V. (2008) 'Fathers' role in the etiology, prevention and treatment of child anxiety: A review and new model', *Clinical Psychology Review*, 28, 539–558.

Boles, A. (1984) 'Predictors and Correlates of Marital Satisfaction During the Transition to Parenthood'. Doctoral Dissertation, University of California, Berkeley.

Bowlby, J. (1969) *Attachment and Loss: Attachment* (1st edn). London: Hogarth.

Bowlby, J. (1980) *Attachment and Loss: Sadness and Depression* (3rd edn). London: Hogarth.

Bradshaw, J., Stimson, C., Skinner, C. & Williams, J. (1999) *Absent Fathers.* London: Routledge.

Brannen, J. & Collard, J. (1982) *Marriages in Trouble.* London: Tavistock.

Brannen, J., Moss, P., Owen, C. & Wale, C. (1997) *Mothers, Fathers and Employment: Parents and the Labour Market in Britain 1984–1994.* London: Department for Education and Employment.

Brearly, M. (1986) 'Counsellors and clients: Men or women', *Marriage Guidance*, 22(2), 3–9.

Briscoe, M. (1982) 'Sex differences in psychological wellbeing', *Psychological Medicine Monograph Supplement 1.* Cambridge: Cambridge University Press.

Bronte-Tinkew, J., Carrano, J., Horowitz, A. & Kinukawa, A. (2008) 'Involvement among resident fathers and links to infant cognitive outcomes', *Journal of Family Issues*, 29, 1211–1244.

Brown, G. & Harris, T. (1978) *Social Origins of Depression: A Study of Psychiatric Disorder in Women*. London: Tavistock.

Brown, G. W. & Harris, T. O. (1989) *Life Events and Illness*. London: Unwin Hyman.

Burgess, A. (2009) *Fathers and Parenting Interventions: What Works?* London: Fatherhood Institute.

Burghes, L., Clarke, L. & Cronin, N. (1997) *Fathers and Fatherhood in Britain*, Occasional Paper 23. London: Family Policy Studies Centre.

Burman, E. (1994) *Deconstructing Developmental Psychology*. Hove: Routledge.

Byng-Hall, J. (1991) 'The application of attachment theory to understanding and treatment in family therapy', in C. M. Parkes (ed.), *Attachment Across the Life Cycle*. London and New York: Tavistock/Routledge.

Byng-Hall, J. (1995) 'Creating a secure family base: Some implications of attachment theory for Family Therapy', *Family Process*, 34, 45–58

Cabrera, N. J. & Coll, C. G. (2004) 'Latino fathers: Uncharted territory in need of much exploration', in Lamb (ed.), *The Role of the Father in Child Development* (pp. 98–120).

Cabrera, N. J., Tamis-LeMonda, S., Bradley, R. H., Hofferth, S. & Lamb, M. E. (2000) 'Fatherhood in the twenty-first century', *Child Development*, 71, 127–136.

Caffaro, J. V. (1991) 'A room full of fathers', *Journal of Family Psychotherapy*, 2(4), 27–40.

Canetto, S. S. & Sakinofsky, I. (1998) 'The gender paradox in suicide', *Suicide and Life-Threatening Behaviour*, 28, 1–23.

Cannon, E. A., Schoppe-Sullivan, S. J., Mangelsdorf, S. C., Brown, G. L. & Sokolowski, M. S. (2008) 'Parent characteristics as antecedents of maternal gatekeeping and fathering behavior', *Family Process*, 47, 501–519.

Carr, A. (1991) 'Milan systemic family therapy: A review of ten empirical investigations', *Journal of Family Therapy*, 13, 237–263.

Carr, A. (1995) *Positive Practice: A Step-by-Step Guide to Family Therapy*. Chur: Harwood Academic.

Cassano, M., Adrian, M. & Veits, G. (2006) 'The inclusion of fathers in the empirical investigation of child psychopathology: An update', *Journal of Clincial Child and Adolescent Psychology*, 35, 583–589.

Cawson, P., Wattam, C., Brooker, S. & Kelly, G. (2000) *Child Maltreatment in the United Kingdom; A Study of the Prevalence of Child Abuse and Neglect*. London: NSPCC.

Cheng, A. T. A. & Lee, C-S. (2000) 'Suicide in Asia and the Far East', in K. Hawton & K. van Heeringen (eds), *The International Handbook of Suicide and Atempted Suicide* (pp. 29–48). London: John Wiley.

Churven, P. G. (1978) 'Families: Parental attitudes to family assessment in a child psychiatry setting', *Journal of Child Psychology and Psychiatry*, 19, 33–43.

Clare, A. (2000) *On Men: Masculinity in Crisis*. London: Chatto & Windus.

Clarke, A. & Clarke, A. (1998) 'Early experience and the life path', *The Psychologist*, 11(9), 433–436.

Clarke, L., O'Brien, M., Day, R. D., Godwin, H., Connolly, J., Hemmings, J. et al. (2005) 'Fathering behind bars in English prisons: Imprisoned fathers' identity and contact with their children', *Fathering: A Journal of Theory, Research, and Practice about Men as Fathers*, 3, 221–241.

Cooper, J. & Vetere, A. (2005) *Domestic Violence and Family Safety: A Systemic Approach to Working with Violence in Families*. London: Whurr/Wiley.

Coplin, J. & Houts, A. (1991) 'Father involvement in parent training for oppositional child behaviour: Progress or stagnation', *Child and Family Behaviour Therapy*, 13(2), 29–51.

Cosby, B. & Pouissant, A. F. (2007) *Come on People*. Nashville, TN: Thomas Nelson.

Costigan, C. & Cox, M. (2001) 'Fathers' participation in family research: Is there a self-selection bias?', *Journal of Family Psychology*, 15, 706–720.

Courtenay, W. H. (1998) 'College men's health: An overview and call to action', *Journal of American College Health*, 46, 279–290.

Cowan, C. P. & Cowan, P. A. (2000) *When Partners Become Parents: The Big Life Change for Couples*. Mahwah, NJ: Lawrence Erlbaum.

Cowan, P. A., Cohn, D. A., Cowan, C. P. & Pearson, J. L. (1996) 'Parents' attachment histories and childrens' externalising and internalising behaviours', *Journal of Consulting and Clinical Psychology*, 64(1), 53–63.

Craigie, T-A. (2008) *Effects of Paternal Presence and Family Instability on Child Cognitive Performance*. Center for Research on Child Wellbeing, Working Paper 2008-03-FF. East Lansing, MI: Michigan State University.

Crystal, D. S. (1994) 'Concepts of deviance in children and adolescents: The case of Japan', *Deviant Behaviour*, 15, 241–266.

Cummings, E. & Davies, P. (1994) 'Maternal depression and child development', *Journal of Child Psychology and Psychiatry*, 35, 73–112.

Cummings, E. M., Goeke-Morey, M. C. & Raymond, J. (2004) 'Fathers in family context: Effects of marital quality and marital conflict', in Lamb (ed.), *The Role of the Father in Child Development* (pp. 196–221).

Dadds, M. R., Schwarts, S. & Sanders, M. R. (1987) 'Marital discord and treatment outcome in behavioural treatment of child conduct disorders', *Journal of Consulting and Clinical Psychology*, 55, 396–403.

Dale, B. & Altschuler, J. (1997) 'Different language/different gender: Narratives of inclusion and exclusion', in R. K. Papadopoulos (ed.), *Multiple Voices* (pp. 125–145). London: Tavistock Clinic Series.

Dallos, R. (2006) *Attachment Narrative Therapy: Integrating Narrative, Systemic and Attachment Therapies*. Maidenhead: Open University Press.

Dallos, R., Neale, A. & Strouthos, M. (1997) 'Pathways to problems – The evolution of "pathology"', *Journal of Family Therapy*, 19, 369–399.

Daly, K. (1993) 'Through the eyes of others: Reconstructing the meaning of fatherhood', in T. Haddad (ed.), *Men and Masculinities: A Critical Anthology* (pp. 203–221). Toronto: Canadian Scholars Press.

Day, R. (guest editor) (2005) 'Fathers in Prison', *Fathering: A Journal of Theory, Research, and Practice about Men as Fathers* 3(3).

Day, R. D., Acock, A. C., Bahr, S. J. & Arditti, J. (2005) 'Incarcerated fathers returning home to children and families: Introduction to the special issue and a primer on doing research with men in prison', *Fathering*, 3(3), 183–200.

De Falco, S., Esposito, G., Venutil, P. & Bornstein, M. H. (2008) 'Fathers' play with their Down Syndrome children', *Journal of Intellectual Disability Research*, 52, 490–502.

Deater-Deckard, K. (1998) 'Parenting stress and child adjustment: Some old hypotheses and new questions', *Clinical Psychology: Science and Practice*, 5(3), 314–332.

Deater-Deckard, K., Scarr, S., McCartney, K. & Eisenberg, M. (1994) 'Paternal separation anxiety: Relationships with parenting stress, child-rearing attitudes, and maternal anxieties', *Psychological Science*, 5(6), 341–346.

Dienhart, A. (2001) 'Engaging men in family therapy: Does the gender of the therapist make a difference?', *Journal of Family Therapy*, 23, 21–45.

Dienhart, A. & Avis, J. M. (1994) 'Working with men in family therapy: An exploratory study', *Journal of Marital and Family Therapy*, 20, 397–417.

Dowling, E. & Gorrell Barnes, G. (2000) *Working with Children and Parents through Separation and Divorce*. Basingstoke: Macmillan.

Dozier, M., Stevenson, A. L., Lee, S. W. & Velligan, D. I. (1991) 'Attachment organization and familial overinvolvement for adults with serious psychopathological disorders', *Development and Psychopathology*, 3, 475–489.

Drew, L. M., Richard, M. H. & Smith, P. K. (1998) 'Grandparenting and its relationship to parenting', *Clinical Child Psychology and Psychiatry*, 3, 465–480.

Duhig, A. M., Phares, V. & Birkeland, R. W. (2002) 'Involvement of fathers in therapy: A survey of clinicians', *Professional Psychology, Research and Practice*, 4, 389–395.

Dunn, J. (2002) 'The adjustment of children in stepfamilies: Lessons from community studies', *Child and Adolescent Mental Health*, 7, 154–161.

Dunn, J. (2003) 'Contact and children's perspectives on parental relationships', in A. Bainham, B. Lindley, M. Richards & L. Trinder (eds), *Children and Their Families: Contact, Rights and Welfare*. Oxford: Hart.

Dunn, J. (2004) 'Annotation: Children's relationships with their nonresident fathers', *Journal of Child Psychology and Psychiatry*, 45, 659–671.

Dunn, J. (2005) 'Daddy doesn't live here any more', *The Psychologist*, 18, 28–31.

Duursma, E., Pan, B. A. & Raikes, H. (2008) 'Predictors and outcomes of low-income fathers' reading with their toddlers', *Early Childhood Research Quarterly*, 23, 351–365.

Dyer, W. J. (2005) 'Prison, fathers, and identity: A theory of how incarceration affects paternal identity', *Fathering*, 3, 201–219.

Earls, F. (1976) 'The fathers (not the mothers): Their importance and influence with infants and young children', *Psychiatry*, 39, August, 209–225.

Egan-Sage, E. & Carpenter, J. (1999) 'Family characteristics of children in cases of alleged abuse and neglect', *Child Abuse Review*, 8, 301–313.

Eiduson, B. T. & Alexander, J. W. (1978) 'The role of children in alternative family styles', *Journal of Social Issues*, 34, 149–167.

Ellis, B. J., Bates, J. E., Dodge, K. A., Fergusson, D. M., Horwood, L. J., Pettit, G. S. et al. (2003) 'Does father absence place daughters at special risk for early sexual activity and teenage pregnancy?', *Child Development*, 74, 801–821.

Erickson, B. M. (1993) *Helping Men Change: The Role of the Female Therapist.* Thousand Oaks, CA: Sage.

Erikson, E. H. (1965) *Childhood and Society.* London: Penguin.

Etchegoyen, A. & Trowell, J. (2002) *The Importance of Fathers: A Psychoanalytic Re-Evaluation.* Hove: Brunner-Routledge.

Fagan, J. (2008) 'Randomized study of a prebirth coparenting intervention with adolescent and young fathers', *Family Relations*, 57, 309–323.

Family Rights Group (2006–8) *Fathers Matter: Research Findings on Fathers and Their Involvement with Social Care Services*, Vols. 1 and 2. London, FRG.

Fatherhood Institute (2006) www.fatherhoodinstitute.org/index.php?id=6&cID=112

Farrington, D. (2000) 'Explaining and preventing crime', *Criminology*, 38, 1–24.

Featherstone, B. (2000) 'Taking fathers seriously', *British Journal of Social Work*, 33, 239–254.

Featherstone, B. (2009) *Contemporary Fathering: Theory, Policy and Practice.* Bristol: Policy Press.

Featherstone, B., Rivett, M. & Scourfield, J. (2007) *Working with Men in Health and Social Care.* London: Sage.

Feeney, J. & Noller, P. (1996) *Adult Attachment.* Thousand Oaks, CA: Sage.

Fein, R. (1978) 'Consideration of men's experiences and the birth of a first child', in W. B. Miller (ed.), *The First Child and Family Formation.* Chapel Hill, NC: University of North Carolina.

Ferholt, J. B. & Gurwitt, A. (1982) 'Involving father in treatment', in S. H. Cath (ed.), *Father and Child: Developmental and Clinical Perspectives.* Boston: Little, Brown & Co.

Finken, L. & Amato, P. (1993) 'Parental self-esteem and behaviour problems in children: Similarities between mothers and fathers', *Sex Roles*, 28(9/10), 569–582.

Fletcher, R. (2009) 'Promoting infant well-being in the context of maternal depression by supporting the father', *Infant Mental Health Journal*, 30, 95–102.

Fletcher, R. J. & Visser, A. L. (2008) 'Facilitating father engagement: The role of Family Relationship Centres', *Journal of Family Studies*, 14(1), 53–64.

Flouri, E. (2005) *Fathering and Child Outcomes.* Chichester: John Wiley.

Flouri, E. (2008) 'Fathering and adolescents' adjustment: The role of father's involvement, residence and biology status', *Child: Care, Health and Development*, 34, 152–161.

Flouri, E. & Buchanan, A. (2004) 'Early father's and mother's involvement and child's later educational outcomes', *British Journal of Educational Psychology*, 74, 141–153.

Flynn, J. K. (1998) 'Mothers and Fathers in Family Therapy: A Survey of Family Therapists'. Dissertation submitted as partial fulfilment of M.Sc. in Family Therapy, Birkbeck College, University of London in collaboration with the Institute of Family Therapy.

Fonagy, P., Steele, M., Steele, H., Higgit, A. & Target, M. (1994) The Emanuel Miller Memorial Lecture 1992, 'The theory and practice of resilience', *Journal of Child Psychology and Psychiatry*, 35, 231–258.

Fonagy, P., Steele, M., Steele, H., Moran, G. & Higgins, A. (1991) 'The capacity for understanding mental states: The reflective self in parent and child and its significance for security of attachment', *Infant Mental Health Journal*, 12, 201–218.

Foote, R. C., Schumann, E. M., Jones, M. L. & Eyberg, S. M. (1998) 'Parent–child interaction therapy', *Clinical Child Psychology and Psychiatry*, 3(3), 361–373.

Fox, N., Kimmerly, N. & Schafer, W. (1991) 'Attachment to mother/attachment to father: A meta-analysis', *Child Development*, 52, 210–225.

Frankenburg, F. R. (1984) 'Female therapists in the management of anorexia nervosa', *International Journal of Eating Disorders*, 3(4), 25–33.

Frosh, S. (1992) 'Masculine ideology and psychological therapy', in J. M. Ussher & P. Nicolson (eds), *Gender Issues in Clinical Psychology*. New York: Routledge.

Frosh, S., Phoenix, A. & Pattman, R. (2002) *Young Masculinities: Understanding Boys in Contemporary Society*. Basingstoke: Palgrave.

Fu Keung Wong, D., Oi Bing Lam, D. & Yuk Ching Lai Kwok, S. (2003) 'Stresses and mental health of fathers with younger children in Hong Kong: Implications for social work practices', *International Social Work*, 46, 103–119.

Futris, T. G. & Schoppe-Sullivan, S. J. (2007) 'Mothers' perceptions of barriers, parenting alliance, and adolescent fathers' engagement with their children', *Family Relations*, 56, 258–269.

George, C., Kaplan, N. & Main, M. (1985) 'The Berkeley Adult Attachment Interview'. Unpublished protocol. Berkeley, CA: Department of Psychology, University of California.

Gerson, K. (1993) *No Man's Land: Men's Changing Commitments to Family and Work*. New York: Basic Books.

Ghate, D., Shaw, C. & Hazel, N. (2000) *Fathers and Family Centres: Engaging Fathers in Preventive Services*. York: Joseph Rowntree Foundation/ YPS.

Gingerbread (2000) *Becoming visible – Focus on lone fathers*. London: Gingerbread National Office.

Goodman, W. B., Crouter, A. C., Lanza, S. T. & Cox, M. J. (2008) 'Paternal work characteristics and father–infant interactions in low-income rural families', *Journal of Marriage and Family*, 70, 640–653.

Gorrell Barnes, G. & Dowling, E. (1997) Rewriting the story: Children, parents and post-divorce narratives', in R. K. Papadoupoulos (ed.), *Multiple Voices: Narrative in Systemic Family Psychotherapy*. London: Duckworth.

Gosden, T. & Kirkland, J. (2008). 'A focus group for fathers with learning disabilities: Using a qualitative analysis to develop an understanding of their experiences', *Clinical Psychology Forum*, 191, 20–24.

Gottfried, A. E., Gottfried, A. W., Bathurst, K. & Killian, C. (1999). 'Maternal and dual-earner employment', in Lamb (ed.), *Parenting and Child Development in Nontraditional Families*.

Graham, H. (1984), *Women, Health and the Family*. London: Wheatsheaf.

Graham, S. (1992). 'Most of the subjects were white and middle-class: Trends in published research on African Americans in selected APA journals 1979–1989', *American Psychologist*, 47, 629–639.

Green, H., Mc Ginnity, A., Meltzer, H., Ford, T. & Goodman, R. (2005) *Mental Health of Children and Young People in Great Britain 2004*. London: The Stationery Office.

Greenberger, E. & O'Neil, R. (1990) 'Parents' concerns about their child's development: Implications for fathers' and mothers' well-being and attitudes towards work', *Journal of Marriage and the Family*, 52, 621–635.

Greenland, K., Scourfield, J., Smalley, N., Prior, L. & Scourfield, J. (2009) 'Theoretical antecedents of distress disclosure in a community sample of young people', *Journal of Applied Social Psychology*, 39(9), 2045–2068.

Grossman, K., Grossman, K. E., Fremmer-Bombik, E., Kindler, H., Scheurer-Englisch, H. & Zimmerman, P. (2002) 'The uniqueness of the child–father attachment relationship: Fathers' sensitive and challenging play as a ivotal variable in a 16-year longitudinal study', *Social Development*, 11, 307–331.

Guillebeaux, F., Storm, C. L. & Demaris, A. (1986) 'Luring the reluctant male: A study of males participating in marriage and family therapy', *Family Therapy*, 13, 215–225.

Gunzberg, J. C. (1994). '"What works?" Therapeutic experience with grieving clients', *Journal of Family Therapy*, 16, 159–171.

Gurman, A. & Kniskern, D. (1981) 'Family therapy outcome research: Progress, perspective and prospect' in S. L. Garfield (ed.), *Handbook of Psychotherapy and Behaviour Change*. New York: John Wiley.

Hagan, J. & Dinovitzer, R. (1999) 'Collateral consequences of imprisonment for children, communities and prisoners', in M. Tonry & J. Petersilia (eds), *Prisons Crime and Justice: A Review of Research* (pp. 125–147). Chicago: University of Chicago.

Hall, F., Pawlby, S. J. & Wolkind, S. (1979) 'Early life experiences and later mothering behaviour: A study of mothers and their 20-week old babies', in D. Shaffer (ed.), *The First Year of Life*. London: John Wiley.

Hardesty, J. L., Khaw, L., Chung, G. H. & Martin, J. M. (2008) 'Coparenting relationships after divorce: Variations by type of marital violence and fathers' role differentiation', *Family Relations*, 57, 479–491.

Harris, K. M. & Morgan, S. P. (1991) 'Fathers, sons, and daughters: Differential paternal involvement in parenting', *Journal of Marriage and the Family*, 53, 531–544.

Harris, T. & Bifulco, A. (1991) 'Loss of parent in childhood, attachment style, and depression in adulthood', in P. Murray (ed.), *Attachment Across the Life Cycle*. London: Routledge.

Hartman, A. A. & Nicolay, R. C. (1966) 'Sexually deviant behaviour in expectant fathers', *Journal of Abnormal Psychology*, 71, 232–234.

Haskey, J. (1994) *Estimated Numbers of One-parent Families and their Prevalence in Great Britain in 1991*. Population trends. no. 78. London: The Stationery Office.

Hawkins, A. J. & Dollahite, D. C. (1994). 'Book reviews', *Journal of Marriage and the Family*, 56, 772–776.

Hazan, C. & Shaver, P. (1987) 'Romantic love conceptualised as an attachment process', *Journal of Personality and Social Psychology*, 52, 511–524.

Hecker, L. L. (1991) 'Where is dad? Twenty-one ways to involve fathers in family therapy', *Journal of Family Psychotherapy*, 2(2), 31–45.

Herbert, E. & Carpenter, B. (1994) 'Fathers – the secondary partners; Professional perceptions and fathers' reflections', *Children and Society*, 8(1), 31–41.

Hetherington, E. M. (1993) 'An overview of the Virginia longitudinal study of divorce and remarriage with a focus on early adolescence', *Journal of Family Psychology*, 7, 79–98.

Hetherington, E. M. & Stanley-Hagan, M. (1999) 'The adjustment of children with divorced parents: A risk and resiliency perspective', *Journal of Child Psychology and Psychiatry*, 40(1), 129–140.

Heubeck, B., Watson, J. & Russell, G. (1986) 'Father involvement and responsibility in family therapy', in Lamb (ed.), *The Father's Role* (pp. 191–226).

Hewlett, B. S. (2004) 'Fathers in forager, farmer, and pastoral cultures', in Lamb (ed.), *The Role of the Father in Child Development* (pp. 182–195).

Hjelmstedt, A. & Collins, A. (2008) 'Psychological functioning and predictors of father–infant relationship in IVF fathers and controls', *Scandinavian Journal of Caring Sciences*, 22, 72–78.

Hock, E., McBride, S. & Gnezda, M. T. (1989) 'Maternal separation anxiety: Mother–infant separation from the maternal perspective', *Child Development*, 60, 793–802.

Hofferth, S. L. & Anderson, K. G. (2003). 'Are all dads equal? Biology versus marriage as a basis for paternal investment', *Journal of Marriage and the Family*, 65, 213–232.

Hofferth, S. L., Pleck, J., Stueve, J. F., Bianchi, S. & Sayer, L. (2002) 'The Demography of Fathers: What Fathers Do', in C. Tamis-Lemonda & N. Cabrera N. (eds), *Handbook of Father Involvement: Multidisciplinary Perspectives*. Mahwah, NJ: Lawrence Erlbaum.

Hoggart, R. (1957) *The Uses of Literacy*. Harmondsworth: Penguin.

Holden, G. W. & Barker, T. (2004) 'Fathers in violent homes', in Lamb (ed.), *The Role of the Father in Child Development* (pp. 417–445).

Holmes, E. K., Galovan, A. M., Yoshida, K. and Hawkins, A. J. (2010) 'Meta-analysis of the effectiveness of resident fathering programmes: Are family life educators interested in fathers?', *Family Relations*, 59(3), 240–252.

Holmes, J. (1993) *John Bowlby and Attachment Theory*. London and New York: Routledge.

Hops, H. & Seeley, J. R. (1992) 'Parent participation in studies of family interaction: Methodological and substantive considerations', *Behavioural Assessment*, 14, 229–243.

Hunt, S. A. (ed.) (2009) *Family Trends. British Families since the 1950s*. London: Family and Parenting Institute.

Jaffee, S. R., Moffitt, T. E., Caspi, A. & Taylor, A. (2003) 'Life with (or without) Father: The benefits of living with two biological parents depend on the father's antisocial behaviour', *Child Development*, 74, 109–126.

Jenkins, J. M. (2000) 'Marital conflict and children's emotions: The development of an anger organisation', *Journal of Marriage and the Family*, 62, 723–736.

Joseph Rowntree Foundation (2004) www.jrf.org.uk/publications/together-and-apart-children-and-parents-experiencing-separation-and-divorce

Jourard, S. M. (1971) *The Transparent Self*. New York, Cincinnati, Toronto, London & Melbourne: D. Van Nostrand Company.

Keen, S. (1991) *Fire in the Belly: On Being a Man*. New York: Bantam.

Kerr, M. & McKee, L. (1981) 'The father's role in child health care', *Health Visitor*, 54, 47–51.

Kilic, E. Z., Ozguven, H. D. & Sayil, I. (2003) 'The psychological effects of parental mental health on children experiencing disaster: The experience of the Bolu earthquake in Turkey', *Family Process*, 42, 485–495.

Kirschner, L. A., Hauser, S. T. & Genack, A. (1982) 'Research on gender and psychotherapy', in M. T. Notman (ed.), *The Woman Patient*. New York: Plenum Press.

Koestner, R., Weinberger, J. & Franz, C. (1990) 'The family origins of empathic concern: A 26-year longitudinal study', *Journal of Personality and Social Psychology*, 58(4), 709–717.

Kotler, T., Buzwell, S., Romeo, Y. & Bowland, J. (1994) 'Avoidant attachment as a risk factor for health', *British Journal of Medical Psychology*, 67, 237–245.

Kraemer, S. (1993) 'Fathers' roles: Research findings and policy implications', personal notes of author, unpublished.

Kraemer, S. (1994) 'Postnatal development of fathers: How do they cope with their new roles?', *Clinical Psychology Forum*, 64.

Kraemer, S. (1995) 'What are fathers for?', in C. Burck & B. Speed (eds), *Gender, Power and Relationships*. London: Routledge.

Kraemer, S. (2000) 'The fragile male', *British Medical Journal*, 321, 1609–1612.

Kraemer, S (2005) 'Narrative of Fathers and Sons: "There is no such thing as a father"', in A. Vetere & E. Dowling (eds), *Narrative Therapies with Children and their Families: A Practitioners Guide to Concepts and Approaches*. Hove: Routledge.

Kruk, E. (1991) 'Discontinuity between pre- and post- divorce father–child relationships', in C. A. Everett (ed.), *The Consequences of Divorce: Economic and Custodial Impact on Children and Adults* (pp. 195–227). Binghamton, NY: Haworth Press.

Lamb, M. E. (ed.) (1986) *The Father's Role: Applied Perspectives*. New York: John Wiley.

Lamb, M. E. (ed.) (1999) *Parenting and Child Development in Nontraditional Families*. London: Lawrence Erlbaum.

Lamb, M. E. (ed.) (2004) *The Role of the Father in Child Development* (4th edn). Hoboken, NJ: John Wiley.

Lamb, M. E. & Lewis, C. (2004) 'The development and significance of father–child relationships in two-parent families', in Lamb (ed.), *The Role of the Father in Child Development* (pp. 272–306).

Lavigueur, S., Saucier, J. F. & Tremblay, R. E. (1995) 'Supporting fathers and supported mothers in families with disruptive boys: Who are they?', *Journal of Child Psychology and Psychiatry*, 36(6), 1003–1018.

Lavigueur, S., Tremblay, R. E. & Saucier, J. F. (1993). 'Can spouse support be accurately and reliably rated? A generalizability study of families with disruptive boys', *Journal of Child Psychology and Psychiatry*, 34, 689–714.

Levy-Schiff, R. (1994) 'Individual and contextual correlates of marital change across the transition to parenthood', *Developmental Psychology*, 30, 591–601.

Lewinsohn, P. M., Olono, T. M. & Klein, D. N. (2005) 'Psychosocial impairment in offspring of depressed parents', *Psychological Medicine*, 35, 1493–1503.

Lewis, C. (1982) 'The observation of father–infant relationships: An "attachment" to outmoded concepts', in McKee & O'Brien (eds), *The Father Figure*.

Lewis, C. (2000) *A Man's place in the Home: Fathers and Families in the UK*. York: Joseph Rowntree Foundation.

Lewis, C., Newson, E. & Newson, J. (1982) 'Father participation through childhood and its relationship with career aspirations and delinquency', in Beail (ed.), *Fathers: Psychological Perspectives* (pp. 174–193).

Lewis, R. A. (1978) 'Emotional intimacy among men', *Journal of Social Issues*, 34, 108–121.

Littlejohn, R. & Bruggen, P. (1994) 'Fathers past and present: Their role in family therapy', *Current Opinion in Psychiatry*, 7, 229–232.

Lloyd, N., O'Brien, M. & Lewis, C. (2003) *Fathers in Sure Start*. London: National Evaluation of Sure Start: Birkbeck College.

Loney, J. (1997) 'Associations between clinic-referred boys and their fathers on childhood inattention–overactivity and aggression dimensions', *Journal of Abnormal Child Psychology*, 25(6), 499–509.

Lovestone, S. & Kumar, R. (1993) 'Postnatal psychiatric illness: The impact on partners', *British Journal of Psychiatry*, 163, 210–216.

Lummis, T. (1982) 'The historical dimension of fatherhood: A case study 890–1914', in McKee & O'Brien (eds), *The Father Figure* (pp. 43–56).

Lussier, G., Deater-Deckard K., Dunn J. & Davies L. (2002) 'Support across two generations: Children's closeness to grandparents following parental divorce and remarriage', *Journal of Family Psychology*, 16, 363–376.

Mahalik, J. R., Good, G. E. & Englar-Carlson, M. (2003) 'Masculinity scripts, presenting concerns, and help seeking: Implications for practice and training', *Professional Psychology: Research and Practice*, 34, 123–131.

Main, M. (1999) 'Epilogue. Attachment theory: Eighteen points with suggestions for future studies', in J. Cassidy & P. Shaver (eds), *Handbook of Attachment: Theory, Research and Clinical Applications*. New York: Guildford Press.

Manion, J. (1977) 'A study of fathers and infant caretaking', *Birth and the Family Journal*, 4, 174–179.

Marsiglio, W., Amato, P., Day, R. D. & Lamb, M. E. (2000) 'Scholarship on fatherhood in the 1990s and beyond', *Journal of Marriage and the Family*, 62, 1173–1191.

Mash, E. J. & Johnston, C. (1983) 'Parental perceptions of child behaviour problems, parenting self-esteem, and mothers' reported stress in younger and older hyperactive and normal children', *Journal of Consulting and Clinical Psychology*, 51, 86–99.

Mason, B. & Mason, E. (1990) 'Masculinity and family work', in R. J. Perelberg & A. Miller (eds), *Gender and Power in Families*. London & New York: Routledge.

McBride, B. A. & Rane, T. R. (1997) 'Child temperament, parenting stress, and parental involvement: Do mothers and fathers look the same? Poster presented at the Society for Research in Child Development Biennial Meeting, Washington DC, April 3–6, 1997.

McCreary, D. (2004). *Men's Mental Health: A Silent Crisis*. Ottawa: Canadian Health Network.

McKee, L. & O'Brien, M. (1982) *The Father Figure*. London: Tavistock.

McLanahan, S. S., Carlson, M. J. & Bzostek, S. (2006) 'Does mother know best? A comparison of biological and social fathers'. Annual Meeting of American Sociological Association, Montreal, QC.

Mendes, H. (1976) 'Single fatherhood', *Social Work*, 21, 308–312.

Merikangas, K. R., Prusoff, B. A. & Weissman, M. M. (1988) 'Parental concordance for affective disorders: Psychopathology in offspring', *Journal of Affective Disorders*, 15, 279–290.

Mikelson, K. S. (2008) 'He said, she said: Comparing mother and father reports of father involvement', *Journal of Marriage and Family*, 70, 613–62.

Miller, J. & Bell, C. (1996) 'Mapping men's mental health', *Journal of Community and Applied Social Psychology*, 6, 317–327.

Minuchin, S. (1974) *Families and Family Therapy*. Cambridge, MA: Harvard University Press.

Moloney, L. (2002) 'Coming out of the shed: Reflections on men and fathers', *Australia & New Zealand Journal of Family Therapy*, 23, 69–77.

Moran, P. & Ghate, D. (2005) 'The effectiveness of parenting support', *Children and Society*, 19, 329–336.

Murray, J. (2002) *Fathers in Prison*.

Murray, J. & Farrington, D. P. (2008) 'Parental imprisonment: Long-lasting effects on boys' internalizing problems through the life course', *Development and Psychopathology*, 20, 273–290.

National Evaluation of Sure Start Programmes (2008) www.dcsf.gov.uk/everychildmatters/research/evaluations/nationalevaluation/NESS/nesspublications

Nazroo, J. Y., Edwards, A. C. & Brown, G. W. (1997) 'Gender differences in the onset of depression following a shared life event: A study of couples', *Psychological Medicine*, 27, 9–19.

Nettle, D. (2008) 'Why do some dads get more invovled than others? Evidence from a large British cohort', *Evolution and Human Behaviour*, 29, 416–423.

Newson, J. & Newson, E. (1963) *Patterns of Infant Care in an Urban Community*. London: George Allen and Unwin.

Newson, J. & Newson, E. (1968) *Patterns of Care in an Urban Community*. London: George Allen and Unwin.

Nolen-Hoeksema, S. (1987) 'Sex differences in unipolar depression: Evidence and theory', *Psychological Bulletin*, 101, 259–282.

O'Brien, M. (1988) 'Men and fathers in therapy', *Journal of Family Therapy*, 19, 109–123.

O'Brien, M. (1994) 'The place of men in a gender-sensitive therapy', *Clinical Psychology Forum*, 64.

O'Brien, M. (1997) 'Space for children: Patterns of family life for children of the 1990s', Professorial Lecture Series, University of North London.

O'Brien, M. (2004) 'Social science and public policy perspectives on fatherhood in the European Union', in Lamb (ed.), *The Role of the Father in Child Development* (pp. 121–145).

O'Brien, M. & Jones, D. (1996) 'Family life in Barking and Dagenham', in T. Butler (ed.), *Rising in the East: The Regeneration of East London*. London: Lawrence and Wishart.

O'Brien, R., Hunt, K. & Hart, G (2005) '"It's caveman stuff, but that is to a certain extent how guys still operate": men's accounts of masculinity and help seeking', *Social Science and Medicine*, 61, 503.

Office for National Statistics (2001)

Office for National Statistics (2005)

Office for National Statistics (2006)

Office for National Statistics (2009)

Olah, L. S. (2001) 'Policy changes and family stability: The Swedish case', *Journal of Law, Policy and the Family*, 15, 118–134.

Parker, G. (1994) 'Parental bonding and depressive disorders', in M. B. Sperling (ed.), *Attachment in Adults: Theory, Assessment and Treatment*. New York: Guilford.

Parker, G., Barrett, E. & Hickie, I. (1992) 'From nurture to network: Examining links between perceptions of parenting received in childhood and social bonds in adulthood', *American Journal of Psychiatry*, 149, 877–885.

Parker, G. & Hadzi-Pavlovic, D. (1992) 'Parental representations of mel-
ancholic and non-melancholic depressives: Examining for specificity
to depressive type and for evidence of additive effects', *Psychological
Medicine*, 22, 657–665.

Parker, G., Tupling, H. & Brown, L. B. (1979) 'A parental bondng instrument', *British Journal of Medical Psychology*, 52, 1–10.

Patrick, M., Hobson, R. P., Castle, D., Howard, R. & Maughan, B. (1994)
'Personality disorder and the mental representation of early social experience', *Development and Psychopathology*, 6, 375–388.

Paulson, J. F., Dauber, S. & Leiferman, J. A. (2006) 'Individual and combined
effects of postpartum depression in mothers and fathers on parenting
behavior', *Pediatrics*, 118, 659–669.

Peacey, V. and Hunt, J. (2009) *I'm not saying it was easy: Contact prob-
lems in separated families*. London: Gingerbread and the Nuffield
Foundation, http://www.gingerbread.org.uk/portal/page/portal/
Website/For%20professionals/Policy/family-policy/New%20research%
20on%20contact/I'm%20not%20saying%20it%20was%20easy%20
FINAL.pdf

Perlesz, A. (2005) 'Deconstructing the fear of father absence', *Journal of
Feminist Family Therapy*, 16, 1–29.

Petersilia, J. (2003) *When Prisoners Come Home: Parole and Prisoner Reentry*.
New York: Oxford University Press.

Peyton, V., Mistry, R., Hruda, L., Zerger, A., O'Brien, M., Roy, C. et al.
(1997) 'Paternal role commitment, child temperament, and the quality of
father – Child interaction'. Poster presented at the Society for Research
in Child Development Biennial Meeting, Washington DC, April 3–6,
1997.

Phares, V. (1992) 'Where's Poppa? The relative lack of attention to the role of
fathers in child and adolescent psychopathology', *American Psychologist*,
47, 656–664.

Phares, V. (1995). 'Fathers' and mothers' participation in research',
Adolescence, 30, 593–602.

Phares, V. (1996) *Fathers and Developmental Psychopathology*. New York: John
Wiley.

Phares, V. & Compas, B. (1992) 'The role of fathers in child and adolescent
psychopathology: Make room for Daddy', *Psychological Bulletin*, 111(3),
387–412.

Phares, V., Fields, S., Kamboukos, D. & Lopez, E. (2005) 'Still Looking for
Poppa', *American Psychologist*, 60, 735–736.

Phillips, A. (1993). *The Trouble with Boys*. London: Pandora.

Potter, C. & Carpenter, J. (2008) 'Something in it for dads: Getting fathers
involved with Sure Start', *Early Childhood Development and Care*, 178,
761–772.

Pruett, K. D. (1993) 'The paternal presence', *Families in Society: The Journal of
Contemporary Human Services*, 74, 46–50.

Quinton, D. & Rutter, M. (1984) 'Parents with children in care. 2: Intergenerational continuities', *Journal of Child Psychology and Psychiatry*, 25, 2231–2250.

Quinton, D. & Rutter, M. (1988). *Parenting Breakdown: The Making and Breaking of Intergenerational Links*. Aldershot: Avebury Gower.

Rabinowitz, F. (2005) 'Group therapy for men', in G. Good & G. Brooks (eds), *The New Handbook of Psychotherapy and Counseling with Men* (pp. 264–277). San Francisco, CA: Jossey Bass.

Radhakrishna, A., Bou-Saada, I. E., Hunter, W. M., Catellier, D. J. & Kotch, J. B. (2001) 'Are father surrogates a risk factor for child maltreatment?', *Child Maltreatment*, 6, 281–289.

Radin, N. (1982) 'Primary caregiving and role-sharing fathers', in Lamb (ed.), *Parenting and Child Development in Nontraditional Families*.

Ramchandani, P., O'Connor, T. G., Evans, J., Heron, J., Murray, L. & Stein, A. (2008a) 'The effects of pre- and postnatal depression in fathers: A natural experiment comparing the effects of exposure to depression on offspring', *Journal of Child Psychology and Psychiatry*, 49, 1069–1078.

Ramchandani, P. & Psychogiou, L. (2009) 'Paternal psychiatric disorders and children's psychological development', *The Lancet online* .

Ramchandani, P., Stein, A., Evans, J. & O'Connor, T. (2005) 'Paternal depression in the postnatal period and child development: A prospective population study', *The Lancet*, 365, 2201.

Ramchandani, P., Stein, A., O'Connor, T., Heron, J., Murray, L. & Evans, J. (2008b) 'Depression in men in the postnatal period and later child psychopathology', *Journal of the American Academy of Child and Adolescent Psychiatry*, 47, 390–398.

Raskin, V. D., Richman, J. A. & Gaines, C. (1990) 'Patterns of depressive symptoms in expectant and new patients', *American Journal of Psychiatry*, 147, 658–660.

Razwan, S. (2006) *Fathers' Involvement in their Children's Upbringing and Education* (for the Children's Society Safestart Project). Abergavenny: Fatherhood Institute.

Reid, W. J. & Crisafulli, A. (1990) 'Marital discord and child behaviour problems: A meta-analysis', *Journal of Abnormal Child Psychology*, 18, 105–117.

Renk, K., Roberts, R., Roddenberry, A., Luick, M., Hillhouse, S., Meehan, C. et al. (2003) 'Mothers, fathers, gender role and time parents spend with children', *Sex Roles*, 48, 305–315.

Riesch, S. K., Kuester, L., Brost, D. & McCarthy, J. G. (1996) 'Fathers' perceptions of how they were parented', *Journal of Community Health Nursing*, 13(1), 13–29.

Robins, L. N., Helzer, J. E., Weissman, M. M., Orvaschel, H., Gruenberg, E., Bruce, J. D. et al. (1984) 'Lifetime prevalence of specific disorders in three sites', *Archives of General Psychiatry*, 41, 949–958.

Robins, L. N. & Regier, D. A. (1991) *Psychiatric Disorders in America: The Epidemiologic Catchment Area Study*. New York: Free Press.

Robins, L. N. & Rutter, M. (1990) *Straight and Devious Pathways from Childhood to Adulthood.* Cambridge: Cambridge University Press.

Rogers, K. & Hazan, C. (1991) 'Attachment in marriage: Effects of security and accuracy of working models', *Journal of Personality and Social Psychology*, 60 (6), 861–869.

Roopnarine, J. L. (2004) 'African American and African Caribbean fathers', in Lamb (ed.), *The Role of the Father in Child Development* (pp. 58–97).

Rosenthal, R. & Rosnow, R. L. (1975) *The Volunteer Subject.* New York: Wiley.

Roskill, C. (2008) 'Report on research on fathers in two children's service authorities', in Roskill, C., Featherstone, B., Ashley, C. and Haresnape, S. (2008) *Fathers Matter, Vol. 2: Further Findings on Fathers and their Involvement with Social Care Services.* London: Family Rights Group.

Roy, K. M. & Dyson, O. L. (2005) 'Gatekeeping in context; Babymama drama and the involvement of incarcerated fathers', *Fathering*, 3, 289–310.

Rutter, M. (1985) 'Resilience in the face of adversity', *British Journal of Psychiatry*, 147, 598– 611.

Rutter, M. (1995) 'Clinical implications of attachment concepts: Retrospect and prospect', *Journal of Child Psychology and Psychiatry*, 36(4), 549–571.

Rutter, M. & Madge, N. (1976) *Cycles of Disadvantage: A Review of Research.* London: Heinemann.

Ryan, M. (2006) 'The experiences of fathers involved with social services departments: A literature review', in C. Ashley, B. Featherstone, C. Roskill, M. Ryan & S. White, *Fathers Matter: Research Findings on Fathers and Their Involvement with Social Care Services*, 13–22. London: Family Rights Group.

Sadeh, A., Flint-Ofir, E., Tirosh, T. & Tikotsky, L. (2007) 'Infant sleep and parental sleep-related cognitions', *Journal of Family Psychology*, 21, 74–87.

Sagi, A. (1982) 'Antecedents and consequences of various degrees of paternal involvement in childrearing: The Israeli Project', in Lamb (ed.), *Parenting and Child Development in Nontraditional Families.*

Sandberg, J. F. & Hofferth, S. L. (2001) 'Changes in children's time with parents: United States 1981–1997', *Demography*, 38, 423–436.

Sarkadi, A., Kristiansson, R., Oberklaid, F. & Bremberg, S. (2008) 'Fathers' involvement and children's developmental outcomes: A systematic review of longitudinal studies', *Acta Paediatrica*, 97, 153–158.

Schoppe-Sullivan, S. J., Brown, G. L., Cannon, E. A., Mangelsdorf, S. C. & Sokolowski, S. C. (2008) 'Maternal gatekeeping, coparenting quality, and fathering behavior in families with infants', *Journal of Family Psychology*, 22, 389–398.

Seiffgre-Krenke, I. & Kollmar, F. (1998) 'Discrepancies between mothers' and fathers' perceptions of sons' and daughters' problem behaviour: A longitudinal analysis of parent–adolescent agreement on internalising and externalising problem behaviour', *Journal of Child Psychology and Psychiatry*, 39(5), 687–698.

Shajahan, P. M. & Cavanagh, J. T. O. (1998) 'Admission for depression-among men in Scotland, 1980–95: Retrospective study', *British Medical Journal*, 316, 1496–1497.

Shaw, E. & Beauchamp, J. (2000) 'Engaging men in relationship counselling: Issues for therapists', *Psychotherapy in Australia*, 6, 26–33.

Sherriff , N. (2007) *Supporting Young Fathers: Examples of Promising Practice.* Brighton: Trust for the Study of Adolescence.

Shulman, S. & Seiffge-Krenke, I. (1997) *Father–Adolescent Relationships: Developmental and Clinical Perspectives.* London: Routledge.

Shwalb, D. W., Nakazawa, J., Yamamoto, T. & Hyun, J-H. (2004) 'Fathering in Japanese, Chinese, and Korean cultures: A review of the research literature', in Lamb (ed.), *The Role of the Father in Child Development* (pp. 146–181).

Ng, S. H. (2007) 'From language acculturation to communication acculturation: Addressee orientation and communication-brokering in family conversations', *Journal of Language and Social Psychology*, 26, 75–90.

Silverstein, L. B. & Auerbach, C. F. (1999) 'Deconstructing the essential father', *American Psychologist*, 54, 1–20.

Simpson, B., McCarthy, P. & Walker, J. (1995) *Being there: Fathers after Divorce.* Newcastle-upon-Tyne: University of Newcastle-upon-Tyne, Relate Centre for Family Studies.

Simpson, J. A. (1990) 'Influence of attachment styles on romantic relationships', *Journal of Personality and Social Psychology*, 59, 971–980.

Singleton, N., Bumpstead, R., O'Brien, M., Lee, A. & Meltzer, H. (2001) *Psychiatric Morbidity among Adults Living in Private Households.* London: The Stationery Office.

Skynner, A. C. R (1976) *One Flesh, Separate Persons.* London: Constable.

Smith, P. K. (2005) 'Grandparents and Grandchildren', *The Psychologist*, 18, 684–687.

Smith, J. A., Braunack-Mayer, J., Wittert, G. A. & Warin, M. J. (2008) 'Qualities men value when communicating with general practitioners: Implications for primary care settings', *The Medical Journal of Australia*, 189, 618–621.

Smith, C. A. & Farrington, D. P. (2004) 'Continuities in antisocial behaviour and parenting across three generations', *Journal of Child Psychology and Psychiatry*, 45, 230–247.

Smith, C. A., Krohn, M. D., Chu, R. & Best, O. (2005) 'African American Fathers: Myths and realities about their involvement with their firstborn children', *Journal of Family Issues*, 26, 975–2001.

Smyth, B. & Moloney, L. (2008) 'Changes in patterns of post-separation parenting over time: A brief review', *Journal of Family Studies*, 141, 7–22.

Snarey, J. P. (1993) *How Fathers Care for the Next Generation: A Four-Decade Study.* London: Harvard University Press.

Staines, J. (2002) 'Health Visitors and Working with Fathers' (unpublished M.Sc.).

Staines, J. & Walters, J. (2008) 'The fathers' group: "A shoulder to cry on"', *Context: The Magazine for Family Therapy and Systemic Practice in the UK*, 96, 15–20.

Stansfeld, S., Head, J., Bartley, M. & Fonagy, P. (2008) 'Social position, early deprivation and the development of attachment', *Social Psychiatry and Psychiatric Epidemiology*, 43, 516–526.

Steele, H., Steele, M. & Fonagy, P. (1996) 'Associations among attachment classifications of mothers, fathers, and their infants', *Child Development*, 67, 541–555.

Stewart, R. B. (1990) *The Second Child: Family Transition and Adjustment.* Newbury Park, CA: Sage.

Stewart, S. D., Manning, W. D. & Smock, P. J. (2003) 'Union formation among men in the US: Does having prior children matter?', *Journal of Marriage and Family*, 65, 90–104.

Strahan, B. J. (1995) 'Predictors of depression: An attachment theoretical approach', *Journal of Family Studies*, 1(1), 33–47.

Swami, V., Stanistreet, D. & Payne, S. (2008) 'Masculinities and suicide', *The Psychologist*, 21, 308–311.

Swinford, S. P., DeMaris, A., Cernkovich, S. A. & Giordano, P. C. (2000) 'Harsh physical discipline in childhood and violence in later romantic involvements: The mediating role of problem behaviours', *Journal of Marriage and the Family*, 62, 508–519.

Tasker, F. (2005) 'Lesbian mothers, gay fathers, and their children: A review', *Developmental and Behavioral Pediatrics*, 26, 224–240.

Tasker, F. & Golombok, S. (1997) *Growing Up in a Lesbian Family.* New York & London: Guildford Press.

Thomas, G., Farrell, M. P. & Barnes, G. M. (1996) 'The effects of single-mother families and non-resident fathers on delinquency and substance abuse in black and white adolescents', *Journal of Marriage and the Family*, 58, 884–894.

Tiano, J. & McNeil, C. B. (2005) 'The inclusion of fathers in behavioral training: A critical evaluation', *Child and Family Behaviour Therapy*, 27, 1–28.

Towne, R. D. & Afterman, J. (1955) 'Psychosis in males related to parenthood', *Bulletin of the Menninger Clinic*, 19, 19–26.

Townsend, M. (2007) *The Father I Had.* London: Bantam.

van Ijzendoorn, M. H. (1992) 'Intergenerational transmission of parenting: A review of studies in nonclinical populations', *Developmental Review*, 12, 76–99.

von Bertalanfy, L. (1950) 'The theory of open systems in physics and biology', *Science*, 3, 25–29.

Ventura, S. J. & Bachrach, C. A. (2000) *Non-marital childbearing in the United States, 1940–1999.* Atlanta, GA: National Vital Statistics Reports, 48, 16.

Vetere, A. (1992) 'Working with families', in J. M. Ussher and P. Nicolson (eds), *Gender Issues in Clinical Psychology.* London: Routledge.

Vetere, A. (2004) 'Editorial: Are We Continuing to Neglect Fathers?', *Clinical Child Psychology and Psychiatry*, 9, 323–326.

Vetere, A. & Cooper, J. (2006). 'Keeping fathers visible: Men and domestic violence and therapeutic responses', *Context: The Magazine for Family Therapy and Systemic Practice in the UK*, 84, 33–35.

Videon, T. M. (2005) 'Parent–child relations and children's psychological well-being: Do dads matter?', *Journal of Family Issues*, 26, 55–78.

Walby, S. (1997) *Gender Tranformations.* London & New York: Routledge.

Walsh, D. (1998) 'Admissions for depression have not increased among men in Republic of Ireland', letter to *British Medical Journal*, 317, 7166.

Walters, J. (1993) 'Sleep management – the hidden agenda', *Child: Care, Health and Development*, 19, 197–208.

Walters, J. (1997) 'Talking with fathers: The inter-relation of significant loss, clinical presentation in children and engagement of fathers in therapy', *Clinical Child Psychology and Psychiatry*, 2(3), 415–430.

Walters, J. (1999) *Fathers' involvement in families with a child attending family and child psychiatric clinics: The relevance of childhood experience, mental health, and current relationships* (Ph.D.).

Walters, J., Tasker, F. & Bichard, S. (2001) '"Too busy"? Fathers' attendance for family appointments', *Journal of Family Therapy*, 23, 3–20.

Walters, M. (1987) Seminar presentation (June). London: Institute of Family Therapy.

Washbrook, E. (2007) *Fathers, Childcare and Children's Readiness to Learn*. Bristol: University of Bristol, Centre for Market and Public Organisation.

Webster-Stratton, C. (1985) 'Predictors of treatment outcome in parent training for conduct disordered children', *Behaviour Therapy*, 16, 223–243.

Webster-Stratton, C. & Herbert, M. (1994) *Troubled Families: Problem Children*. Chichester: John Wiley.

White, A. (2009) 'Big boys really don't cry: Considering men's reluctance to engage in counselling', *Counselling Psychology Review*, 24, 2–8.

White, L. & Gilbreth, J. G. (2001) 'When children have two fathers: Effects of relationships with stepfathers and noncustodial fathers on adolescent outcome', *Journal of Marriage and the Family*, 63, 155–167.

Williams, J. & Miller, J. (2006) 'Gender inequality and the mental health of women and men', in R. Dallos & L. Johnstone (eds), *Formulation in Psychology and Psychotherapy*. London: Routledge.

Woollett, A., White, D. G. & Lyon, M. L. (1982) 'Studies involving fathers: Subject refusal, attrition and sampling bias', *Current Psychological Reviews*, 2, 193–212.

Yablonsky, L. (1990) *Fathers and Sons*. New York, Sydney & London: Gardner Press Trade Book Co.

Yeung, W. J., Sandberg, J. F., Davis-Kean, P. E. & Hofferth, S. L. (2001) 'Children's time with fathers in intact families', *Journal of Marriage and the Family*, 63, 136–154.

Young, M. & Willmott, P. (1957) *Family and Kinship in East London*. London: Routledge and Kegan Paul.

Zilboorg, G. (1931) 'Depressive reactions related to parenthood', *American Journal of Psychiatry*, 87, 927–962.

Zweig-Frank, H. & Paris, J. (1991) 'Parents' emotional neglect and overprotection according to recollections of patients with borderline personality disorder', *American Journal of Psychiatry*, 148, 648–651.

INDEX

Fu Keung Wong, D. et al. 27
Futris, T.G. and Schoppe–Sullivan, S.J. 126–7

gay men
  and fatherhood 103–4
  and mental distress 71
gender of children, differences in father roles 38–40
gender of parents
  mental health conditions 55–6, 70–1
  relationship attachment styles 69–70
  time spent with children 14–16
gender of therapists 108–9, 110–16
  within family centres 138–9
generativity (Snarey) 89
genograms 25, 31
George, C., Kaplan, N. and Main, M. 9, 64
Gerson, K. 82
Ghate, D., Shaw, C. and Hazel, N. 138–9
Gingerbread 43–4, 45–6
Goodman, W.B. et al. 16
Gorell Barnes, G. and Dowling, E. 75
Gosden, T. and Kirkland, J. 137
Gottfried, A.E. et al. 80–1
GP consultations with men 69, 114
Graham, H. 106
Graham, S. 17
grandparents 101–3
Greenberger, E. and O'Neil, R. 83
Green, H. et al. 56
Greenland, K. et al. 68
Grossman, K. et al. 37
group support for fathers 44
group work and fathers 130–40
  content of discussions 133–4
  and emotional education 134–5
  lone fathers 135–6
  participant mix 136–7
  settings 137
  timing 131
Guillebeaux, F. et al. 107
Gunzberg, J.C. 118
Gurman, A. and Kniskern, D. 109

Hagan, J. and Dinovitzer, R. 149
Hall, F. et al. 86
happiness, and father–child closeness 96

Hardesty, J.L. et al. 145
Harris, K.M. and Morgan, S.P. 81
Harris, T. and Bifulco, A. 74
Hartman, A.A. and Nicolay, R.C. 60
Hawkins, A.J. and Dollahite, D.C. 81–2
Hazan, C. and Shaver, P. 70
health visitors, working with men and depression 63–4
Hecker, L.L. 117
help-seeking behaviours (men) 67–71
  and attachment styles 69–70
  cf. women 68, 69–70
  influence of GP communication skills 69
Herbert, E. and Carpenter, B. 108
Hetherington, E.M. 52
Hetherington, E.M. and Stanley–Hagan, M. 95
Heubeck, B. 109
Heubeck, B. et al. 109, 117
Hewlett, B.S. 27–8
Hjelmstedt, A. and Collins, A. 65
Hock, E. et al. 83
Hofferth, S.L. and Anderson, K.G. 16, 19
Hofferth, S.L. et al. 14, 43
Hoggart, R. 33, 78
Holden, G.W. and Barker, T. 145
Holmes, E.K. et al. 10, 130
Holmes, J. 64, 119
Hops, H. and Seeley, J.R. 17
Hunt, S.A. 14–15
hyperactivity, and parental mental ill health 93, 95

Indian cultures and fatherhood 28–9
intergenerational attachment patterns 85–90
  and depression 64–6
  and grandparents 102–3
  impact on quality of marriages 86
  mediating relationships 86
intergenerational violence patterns 154
internalising behaviours, and maternal interactions 96
interpreters, best practices 29–30
IVF procedures, impact on men 65

Jaffee, S.R. et al. 48–9, 143
Japanese cultures and fatherhood 27